AMERICAN HERITAGE

August, 1968 · Volume XIX, Number 5

PRESIDENT JOHNSON STEPS ASIDE

"FAREWELL, A LONG FAREWELL, TO ALL MY GREATNESS!"

HARPER'S WEEKLY, MARCH 13, 1869

AMERICAN HERITAGE

The Magazine of History

SENIOR EDITOR
Bruce Catton

EDITOR
Oliver Jensen

MANAGING EDITOR
Robert Lincoln Reynolds

ART DIRECTOR
Murray Belsky

ART EDITOR
Joan Paterson Kerr

ARTICLES EDITOR
E. M. Halliday

ASSOCIATE EDITORS
Robert S. Gallagher   David G. Lowe
Barbara Klaw   John L. Phillips
Douglas Tunstell

COPY EDITOR
Brenda Niemand

EDITORIAL ASSISTANTS
Mary Dawn Earley   Rosemary L. Klein
Mary A. Hawkins   Joanne Shapiro

PUBLISHER
Darby Perry

ADVISORY BOARD
Allan Nevins, *Chairman*
Carl Carmer   Louis C. Jones
Gerald Carson   Alvin M. Josephy, Jr.
Marshall B. Davidson   Howard H. Peckham
John A. Garraty   Francis S. Ronalds
Eric F. Goldman   S. K. Stevens

AMERICAN HERITAGE is published every two months by American Heritage Publishing Co., Inc., 551 Fifth Avenue, New York, N.Y. 10017.

PRESIDENT
James Parton

CHAIRMAN, EDITORIAL COMMITTEE
Joseph J. Thorndike

MANAGING DIRECTOR, BOOK DIVISION
Richard M. Ketchum

SENIOR ART DIRECTOR
Irwin Glusker

Correspondence about subscriptions should be sent to: American Heritage Subscription Office, 383 West Center Street, Marion, Ohio 43302. Single copies: $4.25. Annual subscriptions: $16.50 in U.S. and Canada; $17.50 elsewhere. An annual Index of AMERICAN HERITAGE is published in February, priced at $1.00. AMERICAN HERITAGE will consider but assumes no responsibility for unsolicited materials. Title registered U.S. Patent Office. Second-class postage paid at New York, N.Y., and at additional mailing offices.

Sponsored by

American Association for State & Local History · Society of American Historians

CONTENTS *August, 1968 · Volume XIX, Number 5*

COVER: Looking romantically languid and young for his years—he was fifty-one when West painted his portrait—Thaddeus Kosciusko was a much-honored veteran of both the American and the Polish revolutions. He had served brilliantly as an engineer at Saratoga, later designed the fortifications at West Point, and helped found the Society of the Cincinnati, which is the subject of the article beginning on page 44. The head and leg wounds from which Kosciusko is recovering in this picture were sustained in the defeat he and his Polish army suffered at Russian hands in 1794. ("Hope, for a season, bade the world farewell," wrote the contemporary poet Thomas Campbell, "And Freedom shriek'd as Kosciusko fell!") The gallant Pole posed for West during a stopover in London on his way to America, where a grateful Congress had granted him five hundred acres of land in Ohio. Before returning to the struggle for Polish independence, he directed that his American assets be used to free and educate Negro slaves, and there is belated historical justice in the fact that West's painting has ended up in the Allen Memorial Art Museum of Oberlin College, the first American institution of higher learning to admit blacks. *Back Cover:* P. T. Barnum spotted this albino family at a fair in Amsterdam and hired them. The family consisted of father, mother, and son; the daughter may be a figment of Currier & Ives' imagination. The print is in the AMERICAN HERITAGE collection.

On the site where Pierre L'Enfant once envisioned a pantheon, the nation's hero

4

re being assembled in the form of a

NATIONAL PORTRAIT GALLERY

By RICHARD M. KETCHUM

In the dreary wasteland of cheap rooming houses and parking lots, nudie shows and pinball parlors, it is surprising to come so suddenly and unexpectedly upon what is surely one of the great buildings in the nation's capital. Only the White House and the Capitol itself are older; only they can rival it in form and beauty and audacious splendor; yet it is typical of the unassuming role this structure has played in the District of Columbia's recent past that it does not even have a proper sort of name. Long-time residents still call it the Old Patent Office Building; officially, it is now the Fine Arts and Portrait Gallery Building, to indicate that it is shared by the National Collection of Fine Arts and the National Portrait Gallery; but mention either name to an inexperienced taxi driver and chances are he will have to ask for directions. Only a tiny fraction of the ten million Americans who visit Washington each year are even aware of its existence, but this neoclassic pile occupies two full city blocks in the run-down, not-quite-blighted Southeast section, and within its superbly vaulted halls will one day hang the collection of pictures that even now is bravely called the National Portrait Gallery.

Here, 177 years ago, at a point roughly halfway between the President's house and the building Congress was to occupy on Jenkins' Hill, Pierre Charles L'Enfant envisioned a national pantheon. L'Enfant, a wildly improvident French painter-turned-architect-and-city-planner, who was chosen to design the new Federal City because his sense of scale appealed to George Washington, was a man of sud-

In the stair hall hangs a loan portrait of Washington; pictures will also be shown in long corridors and small rooms off this hall. The engraving at right shows the building (then the Patent Office) as it looked in 1856.

den whim and passion, and one feature of his grand-iloquent scheme for the capital was that the site in the Southeast area now defined by Seventh, Ninth, F, and G streets should be a place of honor for the nation's immortals. In a curious though far from fully defined way, that is approximately what is now taking place; but how it came to pass, in the contorted course of a century and three quarters, requires a long backward look at the venerable building and its story.

By 1836—long after L'Enfant—Congress adopted a design submitted by William Parker Elliott for a monumental building inspired by the Parthenon, and almost immediately President Andrew Jackson—who believed in turning things over to his own men—appointed his court architect, Robert Miller, to execute the work. ("We have entered a new era in the history of the world," Mills proclaimed; "it is our destiny to lead, not to be led.") When the south section of the building was completed in 1840, it was not, as L'Enfant had hoped, the mortal remains of the nation's heroes that were admitted, but the Patent Office—that "temple of the useful arts," which had been destroyed by fire four years earlier along with its collection of seven thousand patent models.

For two decades the edifice grew and its contents proliferated until, by 1860, it contained not only the Patent Office but also the Department of the Interior, the National Institute, the National Museum, and the latest marble-topped washstands and a cuspidor-sterilizing system. An unfriendly critic might sneer at the building as "American composite, a sort of conglomerated specimen of native growth," but Latimer's Guide Book hailed it aptly as "one of the greatest ornaments of the city." During the Civil War, troops were quartered in the building from time to time, and after the Battle of Antietam, wounded and dying men by the hundreds were laid out on the marble floors between display cases full of patent models and assorted mementos collected by Captain Charles Wilkes in the South Seas and Commodore Matthew C. Perry in Japan. Clara Barton and Walt Whitman ministered to the suffering soldiers there, and Whitman described how "two of the immense apartments are filled with high and ponderous glass cases, crowded with models in miniature of every kind of utensil, machine or invention it ever entered into the mind of man to conceive; and with curiosities and foreign presents. Between these cases are lateral openings, perhaps eight feet wide and quite deep, and in these were placed the sick; besides a great long double row of them, up and down through the middle of the hall. Many of them are very bad . . . wounds, and amputations."

As one of the wonders of the capital city, the Patent Office Building in 1865 was the setting for Lincoln's

TEXT CONTINUED ON PAGE 108
ILLUSTRATIONS CONTINUE ON FOLLOWING PAGES

6

AN
ELEGANT
SETTING

The long, balconied "Model-Hall" (right), at the head of the double curving stairway shown on page 4, is the way the top floor was restored after the 1877 fire. Done in the best American Renaissance style, it was the largest room in the United States at that time. Here, in a wondrous mix of marble, stained and etched glass, mosaic tile, and trompe l'oeil columns, the collection of patent models was displayed until 1932, bathed in soft colors from the skylight above and in the approbation of those American inventors whose bas-relief countenances appear on the walls. In the photograph below, William F. Draper's portrait of President John F. Kennedy hangs in a small, intimate gallery typical of many rooms in the building.

BOTH: PHOTOGRAPH BY PAULUS LEESER

CHARLES COTESWORTH PINCKNEY, 1746–1825

Ætatis suæ 21. Aº 1616.

Matoaks als Rebecka daughter to the mighty Prince
Powhatan Emperour of Attanoughkomouck als Virginia
converted and baptized in the Christian faith, and
Wife to the worth Mr Tho: Rolff.

POCAHONTAS, 1595?–1617

HENRY LAURENS, 1724–1792

GEMS OF THE GALLERY

*The gaggle of southerners on these pages represents
the crown jewels in the National Portrait Gallery's
collection. Considered the finest of them all is the oil
portrait, opposite, of South Carolina's soldier-states-
man Charles Pinckney, done about 1775 by Henry
Benbridge, the instructor of Thomas Sully. But if
Pinckney is the best, Pocahontas is the earliest and
in some respects the most interesting picture in the
gallery. An unknown artist painted John Rolfe's
Indian bride in 1616 when he took her to England.
Known also as Matoaka, and baptized Rebecca, Powhatan's daughter in a stiff Stuart costume scarcely
suggests the child of nature who danced naked before Captain John Smith in far-away Virginia. The
Charleston planter and patriot Henry Laurens also
had his portrait painted in England: it was done by
the American John Singleton Copley in 1782, when
Laurens, who had been captured by the British while
on his way to negotiate a treaty with the Dutch, was
in prison. Charles Willson Peale painted the likeness
of Revolutionary general William Moultrie in 1782.*

WILLIAM MOULTRIE, 1730–1805

JOHN CALDWELL CALHOUN, 1782–1850

WILLIAM TECUMSEH SHERMAN, 1820–1891

FACETS OF GREATNESS

Nineteenth-century America's artistic debt to Europe is evident in many handsome portraits in the gallery's permanent collection. Charles Bird King, who painted the vigorous likeness of John C. Calhoun in 1823, when Calhoun was Secretary of War in Monroe's Cabinet, had studied for eight years in London with Benjamin West. George Peter Alexander Healy, whose 1866 study of General William T. Sherman is reproduced below left, trained in Paris and returned home to become one of America's most sought-after portraitists. Paul Bartlett, himself a painter and sculptor who spent years in France, struck an elegant pose about 1895 for Charles Sprague Pearce, another Paris-educated artist. Bartlett, who sculpted the pediment for the House wing of the Capitol, seems to have been a favorite model for fellow artists: at least three others did portraits of him. A recent work that is now part of the National Portrait Gallery collection is a bust of Rachel Carson, biologist and author of Silent Spring *and* The Sea Around Us, *which was sculpted from memory in 1965 by Una Hanbury, a Washington, D.C., artist.*

RACHEL LOUISE CARSON, 1907–1964

PAUL WAYLAND BARTLETT, 1865–1925

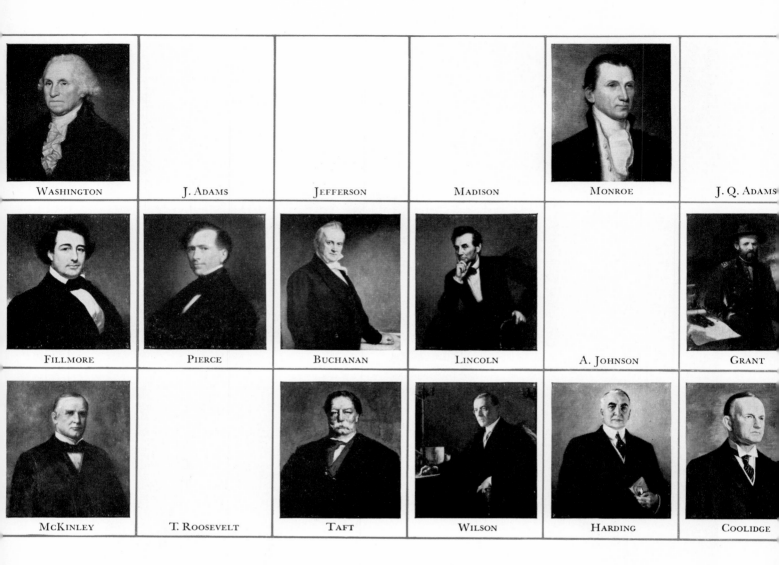

WASHINGTON	J. ADAMS	JEFFERSON	MADISON	MONROE	J. Q. ADAMS
FILLMORE	PIERCE	BUCHANAN	LINCOLN	A. JOHNSON	GRANT
McKINLEY	T. ROOSEVELT	TAFT	WILSON	HARDING	COOLIDGE

MISSING HEROES

Once the real gems of the collection are sifted out, the uneven quality of the remaining portraits is evident. Plainer still are the gaping holes that must be filled if the gallery is to achieve its assigned task of "depicting men and women who have made significant contributions to the history, development, and culture . . . of the United States." Gaps are apparent in a roster of Presidents (above): of thirty-six Chief Executives, the gallery owns portraits of only twenty-three, two of which (Polk and Coolidge) are merely copies of originals. The gallery would prefer replicas (copies made by the artist of his own work) to copies of original portraits done by other painters; it would also prefer a likeness of each President made while he occupied the office (instead, for instance, of having to exhibit Herbert Hoover as a young engineer, or Dwight D. Eisenhower in uniform as SHAEF commander). Numerous portraits of most Presidents exist, of

course; the problem is how to obtain one of each. It is axiomatic that an art gallery does not look a donor in the mouth, but an institution like the National Portrait Gallery must have a firm policy regarding gifts, lest it be inundated with portraits like the one of Eleanor Roosevelt at right, which was painted from a photograph. Yet, as a Briton observed of England's National Portrait Gallery, "It is easier to find a good picture than a good picture that is a good portrait of a good man." Partisans may carp at the gallery's representations of Albert Einstein, Mrs. Roosevelt, or Billy Rose (opposite), but the only practicable means of including certain individuals or of showing them in a kinder light may be to break the ban Congress has imposed on the inclusion of photographs in the permanent collection, or somehow to persuade other museums, galleries, and private collectors to divest themselves of significant paintings or sculptures.

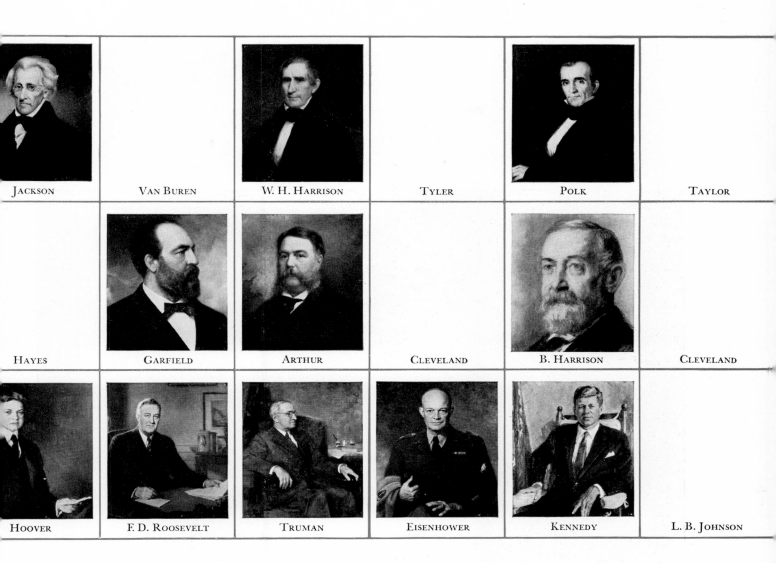

JACKSON	VAN BUREN	W. H. HARRISON	TYLER	POLK	TAYLOR
HAYES	GARFIELD	ARTHUR	CLEVELAND	B. HARRISON	CLEVELAND
HOOVER	F. D. ROOSEVELT	TRUMAN	EISENHOWER	KENNEDY	L. B. JOHNSON

ALBERT EINSTEIN, 1879–1955
by Josef Sharl (1950)

ANNA ELEANOR ROOSEVELT, 1884–1962
by Alta Shore Purdy (1958)

BILLY ROSE, 1899–1966
by Edward Weiss (1966)

MIGHT-HAVE-BEENS

One way the National Portrait Gallery can display the glories it might have possessed is by hanging a loan exhibition of the type of pictures that could have come its way had time been on its side. This is one purpose of the show that will open the gallery early in October, 1968, when the halls of the venerable building will be brightened by such superb portraiture as Sully's head of the actress Charlotte Cushman (1843); Peter Lely's standing portrait of Virginia's Governor William Berkeley; paintings of Cardinal Gibbons (1902) and Civil War photographer Mathew Brady (1857); and Charles Temple's charming silhouette of the poet Emily Dickinson (1845).

CHARLOTTE SAUNDERS CUSHMAN, 1816–1876

SIR WILLIAM BERKELEY, 1606–1677

JAMES CARDINAL GIBBONS, 1834–1921

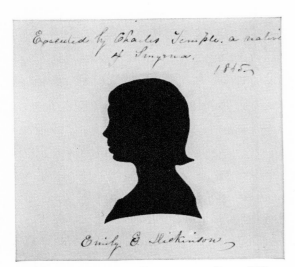

EMILY ELIZABETH DICKINSON, 1830–1886

MATHEW BRADY, 1823?–1896

15

ANDREW WILLIAM MELLON, 1855–1937

CHARLES EVANS HUGHES, 1862–1948

JOHN PHILIP SOUSA, 1854–1932

EMINENT CANDIDATES

These five likenesses, all on loan to the National Portrait Gallery, reflect not only the caliber of art that gallery officials would like to see in the permanent collection, but suggest the range of chronology and the variety of figures to be represented. Andrew Mellon, Pittsburgh financier and patron saint of the National Gallery of Art, was painted by Oswald Birley in 1933. Charles Evans Hughes was Secretary of State in 1921 when Philip Laszlo did his portrait. John Philip Sousa, "the March King," sat for H. P. Waltman in 1909. Harry Hopkins, indispensable aide to Franklin Roosevelt, was sculpted by Reuben Nakian in 1934. Aaron Burr's portrait was completed by John Vanderlyn in 1804, the year Burr killed Hamilton.

HARRY LLOYD HOPKINS, 1890–1946

AARON BURR, 1756–1836

The Bombing of Monte Cassino

The Allied drive toward Rome had stalled. Was the destruction of a historic monastery justified in an effort to break the German line and get the campaign moving again?

By MARTIN BLUMENSON

With an afterword by General Ira C. Eaker

Halfway between Naples and Rome, on a mountaintop and visible for miles, stands the Benedictine abbey of Monte Cassino, serene and benign, apparently indestructible. Of cream-colored stone, its longest side extending 200 yards, four stories tall, with a thick, battlemented base and rows of cell windows, the abbey resembles a fortress. Not particularly beautiful, it is impressive because of its massive size and commanding location. Crowning Monte Cassino, which rises abruptly 1,700 feet above the plain, the abbey overlooks the town of Cassino and the Rapido River, at its foot; to the northwest it superbly dominates the Liri Valley, stretching off toward Rome. It is built around five cloistered courtyards and includes a large church, a seminary, an observatory, a school for 250 boys, a vast library of priceless archives, and various workshops and outbuildings. Since 1866, when Italy dissolved the monasteries, the abbey has been a national monument, the monks remaining as custodians of the structure and its treasures.

The abbey was founded by Saint Benedict himself around 529 A.D. It was ravaged by Lombards in the sixth century, pillaged by Saracens in the ninth, knocked down by an earthquake in the fourteenth, sacked by French troops in the eighteenth, and reduced to rubble by bombs and shells in the twentieth.

To many, the last act of destruction seemed as senseless and wanton as the others. Yet the men who levelled the sanctified walls believed they had compelling reasons. In order to save soldiers' lives, they felt they had to sacrifice an edifice representing one of the great traditions of a civilization they sought to preserve.

The setting was World War II, the stage the Italian campaign, and the destruction an apparent departure from a consistent policy scrupulously observed.

The Combined Chiefs of Staff, the highest Anglo-American military command, had made that policy very clear. Religious, historical, and cultural properties, they said, were to be spared from damage, together with "local archives . . . classical monuments and objects of art." But only if their preservation was "consistent with military necessity."

Although no one ventured to define military necessity precisely, the commanders in the field had made every effort to respect the injunction in the campaigns of North Africa, Sicily, and southern Italy. General Dwight D. Eisenhower, the Supreme Allied Commander in the Mediterranean theatre, assured his superiors that "all precautions to safeguard works of art and monuments are being taken. Naval, ground, and air

In the American reconnaissance photo opposite, the battered town of Cassino lies in the foreground. Above it rises the massif of Monte Cassino; at the top of that, the shell of the abbey itself stands out against the background of the Liri Valley, which leads toward Rome. The value of the abbey's site to the Germans, for observation posts and gun emplacements in stemming the Allied advance, is obvious.

commanders have been so instructed and understand fully [the] importance of preventing unnecessary or avoidable damage." General Mark Clark, who commanded the Fifth Army in Italy, directed his subordinates "to protect these properties, and intentional attacks will therefore be carefully avoided. . . . If, however, military necessity should so dictate, there should be no hesitation in taking whatever action the situation warrants."

In the fall of 1943, although the fighting front was far from Monte Cassino, Italian museum officials reminded the Allied command of the historic and artistic importance of the abbey. Word went out to air units at once: "All possible precautions to be taken to avoid bombing abbey on Monte Cassino."

"Let me see pictures of this place," ordered General Alfred Gruenther, Clark's chief of staff. "Will our ground troops have occasion to demolish it by artillery fire?"

The question was academic until early January, 1944, when Vatican authorities complained that the abbey had been "seriously damaged" by artillery. An immediate investigation revealed what had happened. The town of Cassino had been heavily bombed and shelled for some time and was still under fire because it was occupied by German troops. Since there were "many gun positions and enemy installations in the vicinity of the town," the investigating officer reported, "it is possible that . . . an erratic round hit the Abbey. Any damage caused by our artillery fire would be purely unintentional. . . ."

Despite the clear comprehension reflected in this report, General Clark repeated his instructions. Even though the abbey occupied commanding terrain that "might well serve as an excellent observation post for the enemy," this artistic, historical, and ecclesiastical shrine was to be immune from attack. Except, of course, that this immunity "will not be allowed to interfere with military necessity."

That was the basic issue, and this the essential question: From a military point of view, was it necessary to bomb the abbey?

Having entered southern Italy in September, 1943, Anglo-American forces took Naples and headed for Rome, moving into increasingly difficult ground and meeting stiffening resistance. By mid-autumn the Germans had been in retreat for a year—driven back from Egypt, expelled from Libya and Tunisia, forced out of Sicily, pushed out of southern Italy toward Rome. Now they intended to stop. In the steep-sided mountains around Cassino, they would stand and fight. It was not a hastily prepared position, but a series of formidable strong points known as the Gustav line.

Incorporated into their defensive positions was the hill of Monte Cassino. Inside the abbey, at its summit, were seventy resident monks, about two hundred schoolchildren, nuns, and orphans normally housed there, and several hundred people who had fled the battlefield and sought refuge and sanctuary.

Both warring armies recognized the sanctity of the monastery, but neither had control over accidents. When a German pilot inadvertently flew his plane into the cables of a funicular tramway connecting the abbey and the town at the foot of the mountain, he smashed not only his aircraft but also the tramway. Several days later, when Allied planes dropped bombs on the town of Cassino, they unintentionally released several loads over the abbey. Minor damage resulted. But the monks remained steadfast and calm. They were confident that the Allied and German military forces would respect the building and its grounds.

In mid-October, two German officers drove up the steep hill from the town of Cassino, carefully negotiating the seven hairpin turns over a distance of almost six miles, and reached the gate of the abbey. They asked to see the abbot. Ushered into his presence, they explained that the Ministry of National Education in Mussolini's government had expressed concern over the possible destruction of the abbey's works of art. It would be desirable, they suggested, to remove these treasures to a safe place in Rome, and they offered their assistance.

The abbot, Bishop Gregorio Diamare, was a small and alert man of seventy-eight years who wore his age and his title with ineffable dignity. He found the idea of carrying out the art treasures rather ridiculous. Both adversaries in the war had publicly proclaimed their intention to conserve cultural and religious properties. What harm could come to this holy place?

The German officers bowed and withdrew.

General Sir Bernard Freyberg, top New Zealand commander in Italy, insisted that the abbey be heavily bombed before his ground troops attempted to take Monte Cassino by assault.

20

Two days later they returned. This time they insisted that the abbey was in danger because of the military importance of the hill on which it was located. Although the Germans preferred to fight elsewhere, the officers explained, they had no choice. The hill of Monte Cassino was far too valuable to be excluded from the fortifications being constructed. A battle was sure to take place, and the abbey was certain to incur damage.

The Abbot accepted their offer. On the following day a German military truck arrived, was loaded with art treasures, and made the first of several trips to transport the most venerable relics and objects to Rome. Almost all of the monks also departed for Rome, along with nuns, orphans, schoolchildren, and many of the refugees. The Abbot, five monks, five lay brothers, and about 150 civilians remained. Life on the hill was quiet and somewhat lonely. The sounds of cannon were occasional and distant.

Early in December, the commander of the German Tenth Army in Italy, General Heinrich von Vietinghoff, requested help in solving a problem. How could he use the hill of Monte Cassino in his defenses, he asked his superior, without harming the abbey? "Preserving the extraterritoriality of the monastery," he warned, "is not possible: of necessity it lies directly in the main line of resistance." To fight on Monte Cassino would endanger the monastery. To give up Monte Cassino without a fight would definitely impair the usefulness of the defensive line. For "along with the renunciation of good observation posts and good positions of concealment on our part, the Anglo-Americans almost certainly would not bother about any sort of agreement at the decisive moment [of battle] but would without scruple place themselves in occupation of this point [the abbey itself] which in certain cir-

cumstances might be decisive [for the outcome]."

Field Marshal Albert Kesselring, the commander in chief of the German forces in Italy, gave Vietinghoff an unequivocal answer. He had assured representatives of the Roman Catholic Church in Rome that German troops would refrain from entering the abbey. "This means," Vietinghoff specified when he passed the word along to his subordinates, "only that the building alone is to be spared."

Placing the abbey off limits and drawing a circle with its circumference about 200 yards from the walls, he forbade all troops to cross the line, stationed several military policemen at the abbey entrance to enforce the order, and assured the Abbot that no military installations of any sort would be constructed within the confines of the abbey—that is, within the circle he had traced.

But the slopes of Monte Cassino outside the circle were not off limits. German troops demolished the abbey's outlying buildings to create fields of fire for their weapons, and set up observation posts and emplacements for crew-served guns. There is evidence that they established at least one position inside the circle, an ammunition supply dump in a cave probably no more than 50 yards from the monastery wall.

In January, 1944, as Allied troops approached, the Germans were ready. They evacuated all the refugees still in the monastery except a handful too sick or infirm to be moved. They said they would continue to respect the abbey, but they asked the Abbot to leave. Despite the bustle of Germans digging on the hill and the more frequent and louder sounds of gunfire, the Abbot refused. He had faith in the promises made by both sides.

Recognizing how difficult it would be to batter down and go through the solid defenses around Cassino, the Allied leaders decided to bypass them. They would send a sizable contingent of troops up the west coast of Italy in ships. These men would come ashore at Anzio, about seventy-five miles ahead of the main Allied forces and only thirty miles below Rome. At Anzio they would pose a direct threat to the capital and menace the rear of the Germans holding the Cassino line. Taken by surprise, the Germans would probably have to divert strength from Cassino to defend Rome. And this, the Allies hoped, would enable Allied troops to move forward through Cassino, rush overland, and join the soldiers at Anzio. There they would gather strength for a final surge into Rome.

The plan involved a grave risk. Until the main Allied body of troops could move from Cassino to Anzio, the units holding the beachhead there would be isolated, exposed, and highly vulnerable. But the prize was too tempting. The prospect of quickly cap-

Stunned by the destruction of his monastery, the Abbot of Monte Cassino is helped from a car by General Frido von Senger as he arrives to take refuge at German headquarters.

Looking more desolate than a moonscape, this view of the ruined abbey makes a startling contrast with a picture taken before the bombing. Yet, deep down in its crypts, most of the inhabitants endured the terrible pounding unscathed, as did the tomb and cell of the sixth-century founder, Saint Benedict.

turing the Eternal City persuaded the Allied leaders to accept the hazard.

The importance of Rome was undeniable. Above all, it had symbolic and psychological value to both contestants; and in this connection there was a time factor. The Allies wanted Rome by a certain date—before the cross-Channel attack into Normandy, which was then scheduled for May, 1944. Taking Rome, they believed, would lower the enemy's will to resist and facilitate the Normandy invasion. Thus, a sense of urgency was imparted to the Allied activities in Italy.

In January, General Sir Harold Alexander, the British officer who commanded the two Allied armies in Italy, gave the signal to start "the Rome operation." General Clark, as commander of the U.S. Fifth Army, thereupon opened a massive attack at Cassino. Designed to divert German attention, it culminated on January 20—two days before the Anzio landing—with an attempt to cross the Rapido River and push up the Liri Valley. The river assault, which took place in the shadow of Monte Cassino, failed for a variety of reasons to crack the strong Cassino defenses. The

Anzio landing on January 22 succeeded; but, contrary to Allied expectations, the Germans moved quickly to contain the beachhead there. At the same time they managed to retain enough troops at Cassino to keep their defenses intact and solid.

Now the urgency felt by the Allies underwent a change in emphasis. No longer was Rome the overriding objective. Far more important was an overland advance from Cassino to link up with the American soldiers cruelly exposed on the Anzio plain. And this depended on getting across the Rapido River. Since Monte Cassino dominated the Rapido, giving the Germans excellent observation posts from which to direct artillery and mortar fire, the Allied leaders moved against the mountain. American infantrymen fought a battle marked by extreme exertion and heroism. They got part way up the mountain, but were unable to wrest it from German control. The defenses were simply too strong, the defenders too tenacious. After twenty days of effort, and heavy casualties, the Americans were exhausted and had to admit failure.

Had the ruling that exempted the monastery from

direct fire affected the outcome of the struggle? Some who looked with longing eyes to the high ground that would open the way to Anzio found themselves staring at the abbey. Aloof and indifferent, crowning the mountaintop that represented victory, the building seemed to have taken on a sinister appearance.

Now General Alexander brought in two fresh divisions—one of New Zealanders, the other of Indians—for a renewed assault. According to a new plan that envisaged stretching the German defenses, the Indians would attack Monte Cassino while the New Zealanders crossed the Rapido. The double blow, it was felt, would certainly open a path to Anzio.

Mark Clark was responsible for operations at both Anzio and Cassino. Under Clark, and in direct command of the two-division attack at Cassino, was General Sir Bernard Freyberg.

A New Zealander of imposing physical appearance and impressive reputation, Freyberg was a legendary hero of World War I. He had already sustained his image in World War II by a magnificent record in North Africa and in Crete. Not only was he the com-

mander of New Zealand's military forces in the European theatre; he was also the chief political representative of his government. His dual function was an oddity that sometimes embarrassed his colleagues. For though his military rank subordinated him in the command structure, his political status placed him above his military superiors.

When Clark met Freyberg early in February, he was taken with the New Zealander's commanding presence; his heavy-set figure exuded authority and evoked instant respect. Clark was pleased, too, with Freyberg's energy and aggressiveness. But he also felt a brief twinge of discomfort. Freyberg's dominion troops, he noted, were "very jealous of their prerogatives. The British have found them difficult to handle. They have always been given special considerations which we would not give to our own troops."

Several days later, when the two officers conferred on the new attack, Clark learned that Freyberg was concerned about the abbey of Monte Cassino. Freyberg, as Clark reported the conversation, "expressed some apprehension that the monastery build-

CONTINUED ON PAGE 84

23

In the entire history of the turf there has probably never been anything remotely resembling the 1891 spring and fall horse-racing seasons at the old Gravesend track at Sheepshead Bay in Brooklyn, New York. The extraordinary events that attended the meetings resulted from an economic squeeze play on the part of the Brooklyn Jockey Club, which operated Gravesend. Then, as now, off-track betting was illegal in New York state, but then, as now, it was a popular form of gambling. To keep local betting parlors aware of all the pertinent racing data—post odds, scratches, jockey selections, weights, and results—the Poolsellers Association, a syndicate of Manhattan bookmakers, telegraphed the information direct from the various tracks to the "poolrooms"; for this privilege, the association paid the management of each track $1,000 a day. When in the spring of 1891 the Brooklyn Jockey Club suddenly decided to quadruple the rate, the bookies refused to pay. Somehow they would bootleg the information out of the track; the Jockey Club could go hang.

Thus began a spectacular running battle between Pinkerton's Race Track Police, representing the Jockey Club, and members of New York's remarkably picturesque Gay Nineties underworld, allies of the poolsellers' syndicate. The gamblers were also supported by the Western Union Telegraph Company, which, counting the bookmakers' association a valued patron, threw into the fray several dozen highly imaginative telegraphers.

The ensuing trackside scrimmages went on for weeks, and became so lively and exhilarating that the racing seemed dull by comparison. Indeed, the sports editors of New York's newspapers became so preoccupied detailing Gravesend's warlike side show that a racing fan was often hard put to find on the sports pages the simple facts about which horse had won each race. Each day at the track Pinkerton men, some in uniform, others in plain clothes, guarded the gates, locking them once the crowd was inside. But this was a little like latching the hen-house door after the fox had slipped through. For undetected in the crowd, dis-

The bookies had to get racing data from paddock to betting parlor. All at once some very shady characters began showing up at the entrance to the track

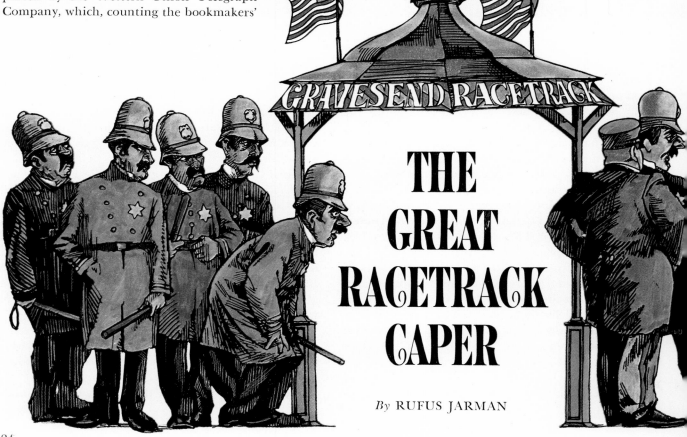

GRAVESEND RACETRACK

THE GREAT RACETRACK CAPER

By RUFUS JARMAN

24

guised as pregnant women, ladies of fashion, gentlemen, or country bumpkins, were a number of gamblers, thieves, dips, touts, and ladies of the evening, allied with the bookmakers and loaded down with all manner of exotic signalling equipment.

As post times neared, they wigwagged semaphores and flags, waved umbrellas, walking canes, and handkerchiefs—one woman even waved a baby—to convey racing data to confederates outside the fences; these in turn passed the information on to telegraphers, who relayed it to the poolrooms in Manhattan, several miles away. Shoplifters brought carrier pigeons into the grounds, concealed in the secret pockets of their professional costumes; released with racing data tied to their legs, the birds took wing and headed for the betting emporiums. But beyond the fences, under the birds' line of flight, marksmen lurked. The Pinkerton detectives were resourceful, too: they captured some of the pigeons inside the park, loaded the birds with incorrect results, and released them. Soon passionate cries of anguish were heard in the betting houses as operators realized they had been paying off the wrong people, sometimes on horses that had run last.

Out at the track, meanwhile, clubbings, fights, and assorted strife swirled about the beleaguered gates. Frequently the crowd was treated to the stirring spectacle of a squad of sweating Pinkertons in full uniform flashing past the grandstand in pursuit of a fleeing poolroom suspect. All this added zest to the sport of kings; the Gravesend track was something like a castle under siege, with the Marx Brothers in the roles of invaders and the Keystone Kops manning the ramparts.

The conflict stemmed indirectly from the Ives Law, passed in 1877, which restricted legal betting in New York state to racetracks. Naturally, the law made betting with bookies more popular. In 1877 Manhattan had only four or five poolrooms, which operated behind barricaded doors equipped with peepholes. By 1891, however, about sixty betting joints were running wide open. A few of them were pretentious and elegant, with mahogany furniture, gilt mirrors, and thick rugs. But most were big, barnlike places with dirty walls, cracked ceilings, and dusty windows. They ran three to the block in the Bowery as adjuncts to saloons, with dollar bets accounting for the bulk of business. All were packed with bettors six hours a day.

So popular had the poolrooms become, in fact, that the crowds at the tracks declined sharply; by 1891, the daily fee the tracks collected from the Poolsellers Association did not make up for the loss in attendance.

The Brooklyn Jockey Club was controlled by Philip J. Dwyer and his brother, Michael, former butchers who had become interested in swift horses when they operated "the fastest meat delivery wagons in New York." Now they owned a celebrated stable of race horses. Phil Dwyer, the club's president, had a droopy mustache and a greater interest in money than in sport. Operating a racetrack in the red made no sense to him, and so, shortly before Gravesend opened its

1891 spring season, he met with poolroom representatives and upped the daily fee to $4,000. The syndicate would not go higher than $1,600.

"The Poolroom King," Peter De Lacy, a top gambler who dressed like a banker, said he considered all betting evil, but if people were going to gamble, it was no worse to do it in poolrooms than at racetracks. "If Phil Dwyer bars Western Union's operators from the track, as he threatens to do," De Lacy told the press, "we'll send in messengers to bring out news of each race. But I don't take any stock in Dwyer's bluff. We defy the Dwyers."

Dwyer was not bluffing. As the spring meeting began, he disconnected all telegraph wires out of Gravesend except one that served the newspapers.

Western Union then rented the old Sleight's Hotel just outside Gravesend's entrance and strung in lines. Once a well-known inn, Sleight's was now a rickety, three-story shell with an old-fashioned cupola overlooking Gravesend's starting post and home stretch. With what they could see from this vantage point, supplemented by the reports of De Lacy's messengers shuttling in and out of the gates, Western Union telegraphers managed to meet their clients' needs with few delays.

The Jockey Club president countered by transforming the track into a fortress garrisoned by 130 private policemen under the personal command of Robert A. Pinkerton, who with his brother, "Big Bill," headed Pinkerton's National Detective Agency. Until now,

newspaper accounts had featured fleecy prose hailing Gravesend's racing as "spirited," "delightful," "splendid," "positively brilliant." Then, on the season's fifth day, the news from the track shifted dramatically from the sports pages to page one. "TRACK A PRISON," screamed the New York *World*. "THOUSANDS PENNED UP ON BROOKLYN RACE COURSE. PINKERTON SLUGGERS CLUB INOFFENSIVE CITIZENS."

The Pinkertons locked the gates, according to the *World,* after some eight thousand people had passed in "as guileless as the wide-mouthed shad which the Spring tides sweep into the fishermen's nets." The *World* and the *Herald* castigated the Jockey Club president as "King Philip, The First" and called the Pinkertons "hybrid policemen" and "chuckle-heads." Both newspapers recounted in horrendous detail the pitiful appeals of patrons to be let out of the track. "I must get to New York," one old gentleman shouted. "I have an important engagement."

"I don't care a damn about your engagement. Nobody can leave this track," said the guard. "Them's my orders."

The *Herald* quoted one "big fellow" who begged, "I am ill; I need a doctor. I've just had a hemorrhage." The Pinkertons were unmoved. A woman with a sick baby pleaded to get out, "but the guards were merciless."

Said an outraged Englishman to an American friend: "You call this a free country, do you? And yet I'm told when I come in here that I can't leave

until a certain hour. That's not liberty. It's tyranny. We wouldn't stand it on the other side." The *World* told of a Kentuckian who drew a big horse pistol and walked out grandly while "every Pinkerton in sight sought shelter." The newspaper added that "the hammering of Pinkerton clubs on other men's heads sounded like the popping of firecrackers on the Fourth of July."

The *New York Times* and the *Sun,* which were against gambling, called these charges "absurd." The persons most eager to leave the track, the *Times* said, "were almost without exception employees of the gambling syndicate or Western Union," which company "ought to be called to account for violating anti-gambling laws."

When the locked gates halted direct smuggling of information, the syndicate undertook fancier measures. Its telegraphers in the hotel cupola had a clear view of the paddock but not of the finish line, so operatives inside the gates performed as "horses": each one held a placard bearing a number corresponding to an entry in each race; after the official results were posted, they galloped across the paddock in the order in which the horses had finished. The watching telegraphers duly transmitted the results. The Pinkertons soon

began chasing the horses, who in their scramble to escape were not always able to flee in the proper sequence; transmitting correct results was a problem. Some poolroom agents now equipped themselves with hollow wooden balls; they stuffed these with papers on which were scribbled odds, jockeys, and results; then they flung the balls over the fences, hoping that associates outside would retrieve them. But the Pinkertons patrolled so vigilantly that few balls fell into the hands for which they were intended; some of them struck bystanders on the head, the *Times* reported, and at least one man was knocked insensible.

The track remained in a state of siege during the rest of the spring meeting. Fighting flared now and then at the gates. The Pinkertons roped off the paddock and continued to chase ball throwers. When the gamblers' telegraph lines suddenly went dead, the bookmakers claimed sabotage and offered a $5,000 reward for capture of the saboteur.

During that summer, while the track was idle, Dwyer had a sixty-five-foot-high wooden fence built, which completely blocked the view from the hotel's cupola. The fall meeting was due to open on September 15. A day or so before the opening, the *Herald*

CONTINUED ON PAGE 92

John F. Fitzgerald put his seal on his city, his times, and a political tribe that still increases. To foes he was "Fitzblarney," but friends called him

Honey Fitz

By FRANCIS RUSSELL

The three-act play runs a century: sixty years from the Great Hunger in Ireland to the election of John Francis Fitzgerald—"Honey Fitz" to Massachusetts—as mayor of Boston; forty more years to see his namesake-grandson, the twenty-nine-year-old John Fitzgerald Kennedy, elected to Congress from Honey Fitz's old district as the first planned step to the Presidency. Those three dates, cut so deep in Boston's history, mark the beginning, middle, and end of a phenomenon as old as history itself—the superseding of one class by another.

Seventy years before the Potato Famine, the seaport peninsula had seen the same thing happen: on a blustery March day in 1776, General William Howe embarked the Boston garrison, and the provincial aristocracy sailed away with the redcoats into exile. Those proudly armigerous Brattles and Vassalls and Dudleys and Hutchinsons abandoned the town to the nonarmigerous class below them.

28

Fitzgerald on the hustings singing "Sweet Adeline." While he was Boston's mayor it was practically the municipal song.

As Boston resumed its pace after the Revolution, the old mansions had new faces in them; sober, hard-faced merchants, men who came to adopt the behavior pattern of their predecessors.

It takes about three generations for a new class to consolidate itself, and it took the grandsons of the Federalist merchants to give Boston its literary flowering and its label of the Athens of America. That flowering came to an end with the waves of Irish immigrants fleeing the Famine.

They were the first mass immigrants to the United States. They arrived in Boston because it was the Cunard terminus, the cheapest distance from Ireland to North America. Their memory of that flight and that passage and the desolation of their arrival remained green and bitter for generations. Over half the immigrants were illiterate; three-quarters had no trade. Five per cent died on the voyage over, wedged in the holds of the stinking "coffin ships." An able-bodied Irish laborer in the city could not in the 1850's earn enough by himself to keep his family. In the depression during the first year of the Civil War, the newcomers starved.

In the harsh atmosphere of Boston, excluded from the common life of the community by both their background and their religion, the Irish formed a society within a society, an emerging Catholic political bloc of their own against the Protestant Yankee oligarchs. During the seventies and eighties the Irish controlled the politics of their street and block, gradually spreading out, precinct by precinct, ward by ward, until it was clear that in a matter of time they would capture the city. Politics came naturally to the Celtic temperament, particularly when all other avenues of mobility were barred to them.

Following the pattern of almost all ethnic groups, the transplanted Irish began by electing their best. Hugh O'Brien was the first Irish immigrant to become mayor of Boston. He was elected in 1884 with the sup-

29

port of dissident Yankee Democrats (for the first of four one-year terms). Not until 1901 did Boston elect its second Irish-born mayor, Patrick Collins. Both O'Brien and Collins were outstanding men, the type one might expect to find as lord mayor of Dublin or Cork or Limerick. Collins, who at twenty-seven won a degree from the Harvard Law School, was elected to Congress in 1882 and served three terms. In the second Cleveland administration the President appointed him consul general in London.

Like his poet-friend John Boyle O'Reilly, Collins tried to pretend away the caste barriers erected against the proletarian Irish. He denied that there was any such thing as an Irish vote, and declaimed passionately: "Americans we are; Americans we will remain." Re-elected in 1903, he died in office in 1905. President Cleveland wrote of him: "In public life he was strictly honest and sincerely devoted to the responsibilities involved." With one almost accidental exception, he was the last mayor of Boston for half a century of whom this could be said.

After him, the practical men took over. The Irish-American politicians, more and more of them now second generation, felt no obligation to observe rules made by the Back Bay ascendancy that had exploited them. The way was open. In the autumn of 1905 John F. Fitzgerald was elected mayor of Boston.

"Honey Fitz" he was called, for his mellifluous rendering of "Sweet Adeline" on the hustings and on all possible social occasions except funerals. The song became his trademark. The taking over of City Hall by this dynamic little political buccaneer was as decisive a date in the history of Boston as General Howe's evacuation of the town. Honey Fitz was the politician who put his seal on his time and his city.

John Francis Fitzgerald's father, Thomas, had come from Wexford, and like most immigrant Irishmen had worked first as a laborer, but by the time his third son, Johnny, came into the world in 1863—four more sons were to follow—he had become the proprietor of a North End grocery and liquor store. The Fitzgeralds lived in a four-story, eight-family red-brick tenement near the Old North Church. Their flat had no bath and no modern gas lighting, but no other family shared the few rooms, and there was always food on the table. By the standards of the Irish North End the Fitzgeralds were well off, nor did the boys think otherwise. Young Johnny came to love the narrow streets and never developed the bitter sense of alienation of his more savage rival, James M. Curley.

"Johnny Fitz" the gang called him; smaller than the other boys, he was quicker with his feet than with his fists. The teeming streets were his self-contained world.

He tagged after the older boys in their games along the docks. Masts and spars were part of his horizon. On winter days the fog would often blanket the North End. In the hot, breathless summer nights the boy lying in bed with his brothers could hear the long-drawn wail of steamship whistles, the clang of the East Boston ferry bell. Johnny Fitz felt the sea in his bones. He never forgot it. "My playgrounds," he said years later, "were the streets and wharves busy with ships from every part of the world."

Early he showed that somewhat officious enterprise that is the mark of the embryo politician. The Fitzgeralds were, of course, regular attenders at the North End's St. Stephen's, and Johnny was equally regular in attending all the parish social functions. So involved did he become in neighborhood affairs, so reliable was he in getting things done, that he was elected president of the Neptune Associates when most of the members were old enough to be his father. This was the strongest social and athletic organization in the North End.

Yet no one could say that Johnny Fitz was Alger all the way. At a time when most North End boys were considered fitted for life with a grammar school diploma, he attended the Boston Latin School, where, as a contemporary of Santayana and Berenson, he received a reasonably classical education. During those years he lost his mother. On graduating from Boston Latin he entered Harvard Medical School, but at the end of his first year his father died, and he had to turn to and help keep the family together. He left Harvard —still a heretical institution to most of the Boston Irish—and took the examination for a job in the Custom House.

He came out near the top of the list on his examination and for the next few years served as a clerk in the Custom House, where he took the measure of the civil service. Then he resigned to set up an insurance office in the North End, specializing in fire insurance. In those willow years he joined every organization that came his way and made his own way to others: the Massachusetts Order of Foresters, the Ancient Order of Hibernians, the Knights of St. Rose, the Red Berry Club, the Heptasophs, the Royal Arcanum, the Charitable Irish Society, the Dorchester Catholic Club, the St. Alphonsus Association, the Catholic Union of Boston, the Young Men's Catholic Association of Boston College, the Franklin Typographical Association, the Knights of Columbus, and others. He was glib and persuasive in casual talk, he was noddingly acquainted with almost all North End families, and he knew every voter by name.

The North End was still a slum. Johnny Fitz sentimentalized it even as he flattered its inhabitants. "Dear old North End" tripped so easily and so frequently

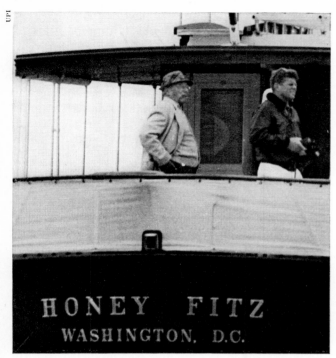

Honey Fitz predicted that his grandson John F. Kennedy would one day occupy the White House. The prophecy was fulfilled, and Kennedy renamed the presidential yacht for the old man. From her stern, in 1962, he watched the races at Newport with his wife's stepfather, Hugh Auchincloss.

from his tongue that his supporters there came to be known as "Dearos." To those who were not his supporters, young Johnny became "Fitzblarney." When he was twenty-six he married Josephine Mary Hannon, a young woman whose good looks became one of the inherited characteristics of the Kennedy clan.

Democratic Boston in the nineties had no consolidating and controlling Tammany Hall as did New York. Power was split among the ward bosses: in the West End, Martin Lomasney—the Ward Eight Mahatma—the most picturesque, the most notorious, yet also the best of the bosses; in East Boston, Patrick Joseph Kennedy, a genial saloonkeeper and the paternal grandfather of President John F. Kennedy; in the South End, at a later date, James Michael Curley.

Johnny Fitz now set out to make himself the boss of the North End. In 1892 he got himself elected to the Boston Common Council. He hired a secretary and turned over most of the insurance business to his brother Henry. The shabby upstairs office became the Jefferson Club, where anyone in the North End was free to drop in at any time. Johnny was at every dance and caper. He kept a card index of everyone in his district who needed a job. At Thanksgiving and Christmas he was on hand with turkey baskets. No wedding

took place in the North End without a prominently displayed present from him. Each morning he scanned the death notices in the Boston *Globe,* and he never missed a wake. He had the actor's gift of easy tears.

In the summer of 1892 he announced he was running for the state Senate. Ward Six's old-time leader died at this time, leaving the young councillor undisputed boss. "The North End Napoleon," the reporters ticketed him, and Johnny Fitz delightedly began to read up on Napoleon and even adopted some of his mannerisms.

Lomasney's announcement from neighboring Ward Eight that he was supporting Fitzgerald made the latter's election certain. It was politician's luck that the Mahatma had an old grudge against Honey Fitz's opponent.

All the political, historical, and sociological strands that make up the Boston ward boss can be seen in the career of Martin Lomasney. Yet of all the bosses he profited least from his position. An orphan bootblack, he started out in manhood as a lamplighter. Eventually he managed to become a city health inspector, and then, as the first step to controlling his ward, he founded the Hendricks Club (named after Cleveland's Vice President, Thomas A. Hendricks, who had once made a speech defending the Irish). It did not take long before Lomasney was master of the West End. His formula was basic: know every family in the West End; help everyone who needed help. The Mahatma's iron paternalism came to dominate the narrow slum streets. There should be a place, he maintained, where a man could come when he was in trouble no matter what he had done. That place was for Lomasney the Hendricks Club. He wrote:

From the standpoint of politics, the great mass of people are interested in only three things—food, clothing and shelter. A politician in a district such as mine sees to it that his people get these things. If he does, he hasn't got to worry about their loyalty and support.

Lomasney's cohorts were on hand to meet each immigrant ship as it arrived. The newcomers were welcomed, given lodgings and jobs, and their names were entered permanently in the Hendricks Club's files.

For Lomasney, being a ward boss was an end in itself. Day after day he held court in the nondescript hall that was the Hendricks Club. His familiar place was behind a battered roll-top desk, a straw hat yellow with age tilted over the baldness of his long head. A drooping handle-bar mustache framed the jutting eminence of his pugnacious jaw. One by one the supplicants came to him, and his appraising blue eyes measured them through narrow, gold-rimmed spectacles. No one would ever have dared lie to the Mahatma.

CONTINUED ON PAGE 76

The lean, mustached American captain pointed to the document on the table before him. Across the table were a half dozen small, brown-skinned men wearing colorful turbans and brilliant silk trousers. At his waist each carried a long, serpentine kris, razor-sharp, made from the finest German steel. A good many companions, similarly armed, stood a few yards away.

Nearby, American sentries nervously fingered their Krag-Jorgensen bolt-action rifles. The captain was obviously getting nowhere with his exotic visitors, who shook their heads and glared defiance.

The captain wheeled and gave a signal to two lieutenants. One of them snapped an order, and two enlisted men trotted out of the captain's tent, one carrying a dead pig, and the other a bucket of blood. The captain knew that his turbaned adversaries regarded pigs' blood as the ultimate defilement; he ladled some from the pail and held it under their noses. He then drew back his arm as if to fling the blood in their faces.

The visitors shrank back. Then, slowly, silently, they came forward and scratched their marks on the paper, pledging somewhat dubious allegiance to the United States of America. The dead pig and the bucket of blood vanished. Captain John J. Pershing's frown be-

Man of war: Pershing surveys his troops just before the assault on the fortress of Bacolod, a vital link in the Moros' chain of resistance in the Lake Lanao district of Mindanao.

came a smile. Thus, in the summer of 1902, a peace of sorts was restored to part of the Philippine island of Mindanao.

It had taken months of patient wheedling to persuade these chieftains to consider a peace conference. Less than a year before, when a well-armed American punitive force had been sent to Mindanao's troublesome Lake Lanao district, these little men with their wavy swords and antique muskets had defied the colonel in command, daring him into a pitched battle. The Americans soon found themselves fighting for their lives. Only their superior firepower saved them from annihilation by these dark warriors, who flung themselves at the Yankee rifles in wave after reckless wave. The colonel hastily retired to the coast, and Captain Pershing, who had accompanied him on the "reconnaissance-in-force," was left in charge of a base camp, with orders to "pacify" the area.

This was still par for the muddling course in 1902, which found America fighting a war in the Philippines —a dirty, vicious guerrilla affair, rife with assassinations and ambushes. At first the generals on the scene and the politicians in Washington had predicted that the fighting would be over in a month or two, but their optimism looked less and less justified with each successive increment in American troop commitment.

The Philippines had fallen into America's lap when Commodore George Dewey blasted Spain's Far Eastern Fleet into oblivion on May 1, 1898 (see "The Sham Battle of Manila" in the December, 1960, AMERICAN HERITAGE). But the United States was not alone in its

U.S. ARMY

Home-front antiw

ever more troops were se

enemy in the Philippi

"Black Jack" w

Pershing

By THOM

interest in the islands. European colonialism was at high tide, and the great powers were hell-bent on grabbing any loose land they could find—the better to justify the enormous funds they were pouring into their armies and navies—and both Britain and Germany had potent fleets in the area. But in December of 1898 a defeated Spain ceded the islands to the United States. America then decided to "protect" its "little brown brothers" until they were ready for self-government.

But the Filipinos did not see it that way. They had been running a fairly successful revolution against the Spanish when the Americans arrived, and in February of 1899 they started shooting up the *Yanquis* with equal enthusiasm.

Americans under Major General Arthur MacArthur scattered the untrained Filipino army in a nine-month campaign. But when the natives shifted to guerrilla tactics in early 1900, the situation became much more trying. To its own astonishment and the world's, America was forced to commit some 120,000 men—two thirds of its armed forces—to pacify the country.

For a while the Filipinos received some outside encouragement; they were especially heartened by the support they won from distinguished Americans. Intellectuals like William James, John Dewey, and Mark Twain, and politicians like Senator George Hoar of Massachusetts, a member of President McKinley's own party, formed the American Anti-Imperialist League to protest the war. They compared MacArthur and his fellow generals to Oliver Cromwell, the seventeenth-century conqueror of Ireland, and to General Valeriano

Weyler, the Spanish "Butcher" of Cuba. The league's magazine urged American soldiers to revolt against their commanders and to refuse to fight. It was denounced as seditious propaganda and barred from the Philippines, which caused still another uproar, this one about freedom of the press.

When the Democratic party backed the anti-imperialists, the Republican administration became keenly aware of the political tiger it was riding. President McKinley issued a directive, effective July 4, 1901, ending military rule in the islands except "in those districts in which insurrection . . . continues to exist or in which public order is not sufficiently restored to enable the Provisional Civil Government to be established." But the guerrilla warfare continued unabated; before it was over, Americans would fight 2,811 separate battles and actions.

On September 28, 1901, some 150 natives of the town of Balangiga, on the island of Samar, staged a dawn attack on Company C of the 9th U.S. Infantry. In ten nightmarish minutes, all but twelve of the Americans were hacked to death with bolos. The survivors managed a near-miraculous retreat by sea. General Mac-Arthur said plaintively in a report: "Each little command has had to provide his own service of security and information by never ceasing patrols, explorations, outposts, escorts and regular guards."

Man of peace: Ever ready to substitute psychology and diplomacy for warfare as a means of pacifying the Filipinos, Pershing negotiates with a Moro chieftain at Camp Vicars.

timent soared as

fight a fierce guerrilla

ngles. On Mindanao,

ght in the cross fire

sland War

LEMING

Soon the troops were singing some rather quaint songs. The favorite, sung to the tune of "Tramp, Tramp, Tramp," began:

> *Damn, damn, damn the Filipino,*
> *Pock-marked Kodiac ladrone [bandit];*
> *Underneath the starry flag*
> *Civilize him with a Krag*
> *And return us to our beloved home.*

None of this highly charged background made Pershing's task simpler at Camp Vicars, on Mindanao. From the high ground on which the camp was built he could look down on beautiful, 450-square-mile Lake Lanao. Around its placid shores were an estimated eighty thousand turbulent tribesmen; Pershing had only about seven hundred men. Compounding his problems was the fact that the natives were Moros, tribesmen who, long since converted to Mohammedanism, were fortified by the warrior doctrines of the Koran. They had evolved their own culture, which encouraged piracy, slavery, multiple marriage, and a fierce fondness for death in battle.

Moro society was still highly feudal; hundreds of local chiefs, called *datus,* each governed anywhere from a few hundred to a few thousand subjects according to the precepts of the Koran. These less-than-amicable characters were not about to surrender their authority to American military men who came announcing that slavery and piracy must cease.

Unlike many of his brother officers, however, Pershing had given some serious thought and preparation to his job. During his first year in the Philippines he had served as a staff officer of the general in command of the Department of Mindanao and Jolo. He had plenty of spare time, and he spent it studying the

Moros. Twelve years earlier he had done much the same thing when he led Negro troops of the 10th Cavalry into Apache country. (That tour of duty later inspired West Point cadets to call him "Nigger Jack" in retaliation for his hard-nosed discipline as an Academy instructor. Softened to "Black Jack," the sobriquet stuck with him throughout his Army career.) His tour with Negro Americans fighting the last rebel redmen in America apparently destroyed any racial prejudice Pershing might have picked up in his Missouri boyhood. Although languages were not his forte—a West Point classmate said the only time he had ever seen Pershing frightened was before French recitations—he had become conversant in some of the Moro dialects. He even learned to read Arabic, and studied the Koran. The swift acquisition of these skills, and his obvious enthusiasm, won Pershing the command at Camp Vicars.

Behind Pershing's efforts lay a clear-cut sense of mission. His attitude is evident in a letter, previously unpublished, that he wrote to a West Point classmate on September 12, 1900:

It seems a pity that the Archipelago has been for centuries in practical possession of people separated into tribes that are so distinct as to have little or nothing in common, and also that no strong hand has been at the head of affairs to guide them by example and by education towards unity of purpose and towards eventual self government. . . .

A government by force is the only one these people have ever known. Those of them who seek official preferment among their own people usually do so by force and principally for personal gain. You know the leaders of the insurrectos and of the roving bands of ladrones are of every blood,—a French mestizo here, a Chinese mestizo there, and so on, nearly all being adventurers whose previous lives would not make very good models to follow. These marauders terrorize the peaceably inclined inhabitants and are followed by a crowd whom they inspire by glibly talking of independence, which means to that same crowd a right to steal, pillage and kill to their heart's content. . . .

Pershing's 27th Infantry and a group of Moros march to war: these pictures, here juxtaposed, come from a rare album on military activities in the Philippines in the early 1900's.

It has been urged by some people at home that the Filipinos should be given their independence. Such a thing would result in anarchy. To whom would we turn over the government? Tagalog, Viscayan, Igorrote, Maccabebee or Moro? No one can answer that any one of these tribes represents the people in any sense, any more than the Sioux represents all the Indians in America. There is no national spirit, and except the few agitators, these people do not want to try independence. They will have to be educated up to it and to self government as we understand it, and their education will take time and patience. It is a grand work cut out for us from which there should be no shirking.

In this spirit, Pershing set out to convince the local datus that he was the Moros' friend. He made it clear that unlike the Spanish, the Americans had no desire to convert them to Christianity. While other officers were applying the "civilize 'em with a Krag" philosophy elsewhere in the islands, Pershing urged the datus to take up farming.

On the Fourth of July, 1902, the captain astonished his men by inviting seven hundred nearby Moros to visit Camp Vicars; the fascinated guests watched the Americans play a strange game in which one man threw a ball at another who defended himself with a bat. Then the natives and soldiers shared the best supper the Army commissary could supply.

This was truly revolutionary stuff in 1902, when the British sahib attitude toward colonials—separate and unequal—was considered the apotheosis of military wisdom. It was well that Pershing blended diplomacy with soldiering to the extent he did, because back home the anti-imperialists in Congress had forced the administration to hold a series of hearings on the conduct of the war. Although the Senate Foreign Relations Committee chairman, Henry Cabot Lodge, did his best to keep hostile witnesses at bay, opposition senators produced grisly testimony from Army court-martial records. The nation heard about such cruelties as the "water torture," which involved pouring gallons of water down a guerrilla's throat to make him talk, and about the foul-ups that led to the starvation of hundreds of civilians in American "reconcentration camps" on Samar. The hearings were a source of growing embarrassment for the administration. A noted American historian, John Holladay Latané, looked through the 3,000 pages of testimony and called it a "humiliating record." In an emotional speech Senator Hoar predicted that the Philippines would never surrender, that the United States could not win the war, and that the conflict would last three hundred years.

On Mindanao, Pershing may have had similar thoughts. His peace preaching was failing to impress some of the more powerful datus. By night they sent their most daring warriors down to the perimeter of Camp Vicars, where they sniped at American sentries, beat tom-toms, and howled insults. "There was not a tent in the camp that had no bullet holes," Pershing later said.

Around the camp was a network of small outposts, and these were favorite targets of the infiltrators. When a Moro got close enough to make a final rush, nothing less than a bullet in the heart or brain could stop him. This was especially true of a *juramentado,* as the Americans, like the Spanish before them, called a Moro who had sworn a sacred oath to kill as many Christians as possible.

Pershing put his men on maximum alert. "No fires, no lights and no smoking will be allowed by outposts," he ordered. "Conversation will be in low tones. Outposts should be moved to a new position just after dark, and on moonlight nights after the moon goes down." Sentries were told to shoot anything that moved at night, except along carefully prescribed trails. One corporal almost killed a lieutenant who strayed off the specified route; Pershing praised the corporal for doing his job.

CONTINUED ON PAGE 101

Captain Newton, immensely proud of his new steam
frigate, was enjoying an excellent dinner ashore. Then
a strange glow began to light the sky over Gibraltar

A Warm

By SCARRITT ADAMS

MARINERS MUSEUM

Evening at the Rock

Captain John Thomas Newton, U.S.N., was greatly annoyed one day in 1829 when he was called away from a dinner party at the Brooklyn Navy Yard. His ship, *Fulton I*, was on fire. It blew up. His new gunner had taken an open light into the powder magazine. Although Newton admittedly had promulgated no safety orders, he thought that nobody in his right mind, with or without orders, would be foolhardy enough to take an open light into such a place. The unfortunate gunner was killed in the explosion; the Captain was court-martialled. However, he was acquitted, as indeed he felt he should have been. The trial had been just one of those troublesome formalities that captains have to go through on such occasions. Nevertheless, he could not quite forget that the *Fulton I* was the very first steam warship ever built, and though her engines had long since been removed and she was merely a hulk used to train seamen for sailing ships-of-war, she was nevertheless an important naval artifact, and he had been entrusted with her care.

But all that was fourteen years ago. Now, on a Saturday evening in August of 1843, Captain Newton was at another dinner party, this time at the American consul's house in Gibraltar. His magnificent new command, the United States steam frigate *Missouri*, the most modern of warships, rode proudly at anchor in the harbor for all to see and admire. How calm it was on this evening. How secure the ship was, with his experienced executive officer out there in charge of the routine coaling operation. Surely no memory of that shocking time when he had been called from dinner at the Brooklyn Navy Yard disturbed Newton in this pleasant situation. He had, in fact, not a worry in the world. And yet—there was a whisper of motion, a nothing, yet something. Now the whisper became audible. The town was coming alive. People were running. Then came a knock at the door.

The impressive size of her paddle wheels and smokestack added to the spectacle as the Missouri flamed to the skies. Her terrified mascot, Bess the bear, perched near the end of the spanker boom (far left), refusing rescuers' appeals.

Only two weeks ago they had left Norfolk. It was a far from ordinary departure. The *Missouri* was out to make a record—to be the first steam warship to cross the Atlantic. They were taking along Caleb Cushing, a top-drawer diplomat, who would attempt to negotiate the first American commercial treaty with China. The President of the United States came aboard for an inspection. In the midst of all this bustle hardly anyone noticed the routine return of the ship's boat from the navy yard with last-minute engineering stores, including two glass demijohns of turpentine.

President John Tyler remained on board a few hours to observe the crew working the ship and to watch her twenty-eight-foot paddle wheels thresh powerfully through the waters of Hampton Roads. At Old Point Comfort he disembarked, knowing that if all went well this 229-foot vessel was on her way to add luster to his Navy.

Captain Newton could not help but think this was an auspicious occasion; he would be the hero of a historic episode. Even if his luck did not hold and his engines failed him, the ship was also fitted out as a full-rigged sailing vessel complete with masts, yards, and sails; they could reach their destination safely and try for the record another time.

The engineers busied themselves stowing away those last-minute engineering stores. Where, for instance, should they put the two glass demijohns of turpentine? Why not put them in that catchall, the starboard engineer's storeroom, easy of access because it was never locked, the hasp on the door having long since been broken off? Here, amidst an indescribable mess of hemp, spare fire hose and oil cans, shelves of heavy tools and spare parts, all mixed up together, the demijohns would never be noticed by Lieutenant Faron, the acting engineer officer. The men well knew that had the regular engineer officer been on board he would have made them pour the turpentine into metal containers and stow it carefully in the safe forehold.

From the maintop a tame bear named Bess, the ship's pet and mascot, a talisman of good luck, looked down over all this activity with serene satisfaction. At length all hands were settled down for the voyage—Captain Newton, Cushing, Bess, the engineers, and the deck force. While the engineers concentrated on the smooth performance of the engine and its coal-gobbling copper boilers, on which the whole success of the record-making trip depended, the executive officer, Lieutenant Simon Bissell, put in motion the watches, drills, and exercises prescribed as standard sea routine. On Mondays there were battle stations; on Tuesdays, Wednesdays, and Thursdays, exercises at small arms and guns. On Fridays, according to regulations, there

should have been fire drills. The men would rig the two force pumps, run out the hoses, man the buckets. But on this trip drills were dispensed with, for reasons not at all clear.

On August 18 the *Missouri* put in to Fayal, in the Azores, to load fresh provisions, water, and two hundred tons of coal. The crew dickered with the dozens of bumboats surrounding the ship, lured on by offers of fresh fruit and vegetables in exchange for old clothes and empty bottles. Men, women, children, and dogs swarmed on board from the bumboats. The bear, in the forefront of those dickering for fruit, simply seized a whole basket of delightful-looking grapes and made off, followed by the vendor in close pursuit. When he got too close, Bess, in a rather unladylike gesture, snatched off the seat of his pants. The crew did not intercede; superstitious as sailors are, they thought it better to be on the side of their own mascot. If no ill befell her, none would befall them. Besides, Bess, who had a record of previous sea duty in the U.S.S. *Ontario,* was entitled to the respect accorded any good shipmate.

The uniforms of the sailors were filthy after loading coal at Fayal, and the men were ordered to scrub their clothes. Then, when the boatswain's mate piped "All hands trice up scrubbed and washed clothing," the men tied their laundry to a jackstay, which was stretched aloft between Bess's maintop and the mizzentop, for drying. But the coal-burning furnaces deep below decks neither knew nor cared about those two hundred pieces of clean white clothing triced up in the rigging, as they unremittingly belched up smoke, unconsumed bits of coal, soot, and cinders. The natural draft carried the debris up the thirty-foot-tall smokestack, and if a few bits fell on the scrubbed and washed clothing, it was all in the day's work of a steam warship.

But the cinders were coming up a little faster than usual, and their quick ascent hardly gave them time to cool off. Indeed, a few still glowed red as they showered down onto the clothes and the furled sails. Little burn holes began to appear, then small flames and puffs of smoke. The cotton clothes, dry in the fresh breeze, were in flames.

The situation looked bad. The *Missouri*'s luck seemed to be running out, with Gibraltar and their great record-to-be only a day's run away. Lieutenant Bissell rushed up to the spar deck, saw the clothes on fire, and peremptorily ordered the men to get the clothesline down so that the rigging itself would not go up in flames. This interference annoyed Lieutenant Simon Blunt, the officer of the deck, because the men began running all over the place just when he was methodically assigning them individually to their fire stations—which he had to do then and there, because no standard fire bill had been posted. But eventually the sailors managed to get the clothes-line down, removing the threat to the rigging. Luck was with them. The storm of hot cinders abated, and the ship was saved.

On that breezy August 25, while the *Missouri* made her approach to Gibraltar under the slender crescent of a new moon, Captain Newton relished the bold contours of the historic "Rock"—walled, ringed with many-gunned batteries, rising abruptly to the crown of Ape Hill. He had made it. The record was his. In the harbor, Her Majesty's seventy-four-gun battleship *Malabar* stood guard. Newton could make out the red light on the Old Mole and the green light on the New Mole as the *Missouri* coasted into her anchorage —a little too far inside the five-fathom curve for safety, thought the crew of the British steam vessel *Locust*. She might run aground, or at least be endangered on a lee shore.

With the leadsmen in the chains chanting "By the mark five," the *Missouri* came to anchor. At that moment she cleared the bottom by nine feet, but as her anchor chain paid out she swung inshore until there was only five feet of clear water under her keel. Regardless of the *Locust*'s criticism, the *Missouri* was safely anchored. Her luck had held for the second time in as many days, each occasion being closer to disaster than anyone seemed to realize. For the super-stitious, however, events happen in threes. Still to come was a third trial of the *Missouri*'s luck that would join her, the *Malabar*, and the *Locust* in a triad of association quite unsuspected by any of them.

Saturday started off with Captain Sir George Sartori-ous of H.M.S. *Malabar* and the captain of the *Locust* visiting the *Missouri* to congratulate Captain Newton and to admire her ten-inch cannon and her engine with its six-foot cylinder. Dockyard boats brought casks of fresh water from the naval tanks a mile away at Rosario Bay. It was a day of many noisy ceremonies. At 10 A.M. the *Missouri* fired a seventeen-gun salute to the governor, Sir Robert T. Wilson. The dockyard replied gun for gun. At noon the *Malabar* fired a twenty-one-gun royal salute to Prince Albert, consort of young Queen Victoria, this being his birthday. And there would be more guns fired as the day wore on to its climax, some on purpose, some not.

There were a few practical things to be done while the *Missouri* was in port. The big steam engine needed overhauling after the strenuous voyage, and the en-gineers addressed themselves to that. But mainly there was coal to be got on board. Two large coal barges came alongside, manned by gangs of Spanish laborers. The boatswain's mate rigged "yard and stay" for whipping the heavy bags on board. Men in the bunkers pushed the coal back into the inner recesses of those dank regions. Topside it was a lovely day, the usual seventy-seven degrees, with a mere zephyr of a breeze from the east; but in the bunkers there was very little air at all, and the temperature seemed twice seventy-seven. What a combustible mixture all that fine coal dust made. Luckily there was nobody around with an open lamp. Or was there?

The day edged inexorably to its finish. The coal bags whipped on full, returned to the barges empty. The procession of water boats contin-ued. Visitors came and went. By 5 P.M. the breeze had dropped altogether. It was party night. Cushing, Cap-tain Newton, and the purser, Rodman Price, went ashore for dinner with Mr. Horatio Sprague, the Amer-ican consul. The sun set at exactly three and one-quarter minutes past six. The *Locust* and the *Malabar* hoisted their boats in; they would not be likely to need them. Bess came down from the maintop for her dinner in the galley of the Missouri. It was the end of the week. Tomorrow, Sunday, would be "holiday" routine. At 7:20 the dockyard gun fired yet again, marking the end of the day. Guards closed the Waterport Gate, and the double-arched Southgate, and all the other gates, securing the bastion of empire for the night.

Nevertheless, work continued in the engine room of the *Missouri*, dimly lighted by the safe if inefficient globe lanterns bracketed to the bulkheads. In this per-vasive gloom a small group of engineers labored might-ily over the big main cylinder. They had gotten to the point where they were putting it back together. John Allen was bolting on the cylinder head. Fireman Alfred Clum was tying on the felt packing around the outside of the cylinder and steam chest, securing the twine to the bolts so it would hold the felt in place. William Wilkins was helping them. They were doing the best they could in the absence of an officer who should have been supervising their work but who for reasons best known to himself was not there.

In spite of the globe lanterns, it was so dark that they could not see what they were doing. So they brought in a couple of open lights which, though for-bidden, nevertheless were often used and were essen-tial if the work was to be completed. They set one of these open lights on the valve stem guide, and Clum held the other so that Allen could see the bolts.

At this point John Sutton, the engineer-storekeeper, headed for the starboard engineer's storeroom, which was just above the engine room, to get a beam scale for weighing coal. Entering this twelve-by-twelve cubi-cle, he stepped onto the loose, removable floor boards

CONTINUED ON PAGE 104

Into one famous short story Ernest Hemingway threw "the material of four novels."

The Slopes of Kilimanjaro

By CARLOS BAKER

In August, 1935, Ernest Hemingway completed the first draft of a story about a writer who died of gangrene on a hunting trip in what was then Tanganyika. The non-fiction "novel," *Green Hills of Africa*, was already in press and due for publication in October. But the book had not used up all the material which Hemingway had accumulated in the course of his shooting safari of January and February, 1934. The new story was an attempt to present some more of what he knew, or could imagine, in fictional form. As was his custom, he put the handwritten sheets away in his desk to settle and objectify. Eight months later, on a fishing trip to Cuba, he re-examined his first draft, modified it somewhat, got it typed, and gave the typescript one final working over. Then he mailed it to Arnold Gingrich for publication in *Esquire* magazine in August, 1936, exactly a year after its inception. Although he had sweated mightily over the title, as he commonly did with all his titles, his ultimate choice displayed the true romantic luminosity. It was called "The Snows of Kilimanjaro."

The new story was curiously and subtly connected with Henry David Thoreau's *Walden*. Thoreau had lately been in Hemingway's consciousness. "There is one [author] at that time [of the nineteenth century] that is supposed to be really good," he had asserted in *Green Hills of Africa*. "I cannot tell you about it [*Walden*] because I have not yet been able to read it. But that means nothing because I cannot read other naturalists unless they are being extremely accurate and not literary. . . . Maybe I'll be able to [read it] later."

If he ever read the second chapter of *Walden*, "Where I Lived and What I Lived For," Hemingway would certainly have been struck by Thoreau's statement about his reasons for the sojourn at Walden Pond. He took to the woods in order "to live deliberately, to front only the essential facts of life." He wanted to learn the lore of nature as early as pos-

ilimanjaro is a snow-covered mountain 19,710 feet high . . . the highest mountain in Africa. . . . Close to the western summit re is the dried and frozen carcass of a leopard. No one has explained what the leopard was seeking at that altitude."

sible so that he would not reach the point of dying only to discover that he "had not lived" in any real sense at all. It is of course a far cry from Thoreau's asceticism to Hemingway's aggressive hedonism. Yet the passage from *Walden*, slightly modified, embodies the theme of "The Snows of Kilimanjaro." For Hemingway's protagonist, Harry, dying of an infection on the plains of Africa, is made to reflect bitterly upon his failure to set down the results of his experience of life in the forms of fiction. Although Hemingway wisely changed his mind before the story appeared, it is a curious fact that his original name for the dying writer in "The Snows" was Henry Walden.

The revised typescript of the story was garnished with a pair of epigraphs, neither of them from Thoreau, but both from "other naturalists." One was drawn from a remarkable book called *Speak to the Earth: Wanderings and Reflections among Elephants and Mountains* (1935). Its author was a naturalized Englishwoman named Vivienne de Watteville, an exact contemporary of Hemingway's, a friend of Edith Wharton's, and a Fellow of the Royal Geographical Society. She was the daughter of Bernard de Watteville, a distinguished Swiss naturalist from Berne. She had been orphaned at the age of twenty-four when her father was mauled to death by an African lion. She had been with him when he died

Ernest Hemingway at thirty-four, happily seeking kudos in kudus' horns on his first African hunting trip. The expedition took place in 1934.

and subsequently wrote a book called *Out in the Blue*, based on her diaries from that safari. She returned to Africa again four years later, recording her adventures in a second volume, *Speak to the Earth*. There Miss de Watteville wrote of her determination to climb Mount Kilimanjaro. An adviser who had already made the ascent drew her a rough map of the trail up the mountain and told her that she "could pick up a guide and porters at Moshi." "This," she said, "fired me more than ever to make the attempt. I had, of course, no climbing outfit with me; but the difficulties, he said, were not in the actual climbing. It was a long grind, and success depended not on skill but on one's ability to withstand the high altitude. His parting words were that I must make the attempt soon, before there was any risk of the rains setting in."

Hemingway's second epigraph, composed by him-

self, stated simply that "Kilimanjaro is a snow-covered mountain 19,710 feet high, and is said to be the highest mountain in Africa. Its western summit is called the Masai 'Ngàje Ngài,' The House of God. Close to the western summit there is the dried and frozen carcass of a leopard. No one has explained what the leopard was seeking at that altitude." Hemingway had gleaned his facts from the guidebooks he had used in preparing for his trip to Kenya and Tanganyika. He had heard the story of the leopard (whose carcass was still there in 1967) from Philip Percival, his white hunter, during an evening's conversation on safari in 1934.

The two epigraphs had in common the idea of immense height. Both Miss de Watteville's anonymous adviser and the example of the dead leopard indicated that the chief problem for the mountaineer on Kibo Peak of Kilimanjaro was "one's ability to withstand the high altitude." In the story, Hemingway's hero was obliged to confront the fact that never in his life had he attempted to climb that high. His bitterness arose from the realization that he was now literally rotting to death without ever having attained the heights of literary achievement to which he had once aspired. In the end, Ernest deleted the epigraph from Vivienne de Watteville, retaining the one he had himself composed.

Harry tries to assuage his bitterness by making a scapegoat of his pleasant wife, Helen. He blames her wealth for his own aesthetic decay. Because of it he has followed a life of ease and sloth instead of realizing his former ambition to be a great writer. More than twenty years after the story first appeared, Hemingway explained how he had arrived at his portraits of Helen and Harry and his conception of the central theme. "If you are interested in how you get the idea for a story," he wrote, "this is how it was." On returning to New York after the African trip early in April, 1934, he was met at the pier by ship news reporters who queried him about his future plans. He told them that he was going to work until he had accumulated enough money to go back to Africa. When the story appeared in the newspapers next morning, "a really nice and really fine and really rich woman" invited him to tea. After "a few drinks," she said that she "had read in the papers about the project." She was unable to see any reason for delay. "She and my wife [Pauline] and I could go to Africa any time and money was only something to be used intelligently for the best enjoyment of good people." The offer struck Ernest as "sincere and fine and good," and he liked the lady "very much." But for various reasons he felt obliged to decline her invitation.

Back in Key West he began to reflect upon what might have happened to someone like himself, whose defects he knew, if he had accepted the offer. Out of these reflections gradually arose a portrait of the lady, whom he named Helen, and one of Harry, the dying writer, to whom she was married. To describe the dying part was no problem to Hemingway. He had been through all that, said he, early, middle, and late. So he invented someone who could not sue him, which was himself, speculated on how he would have turned out under the circumstances, and then put into one short story the material of four novels. He made up the man and the woman, loaded his story with personal and imagined memoirs, and found that even with this load (the heaviest, he thought, that any short story had ever carried) the story still managed to take off and fly. As for the leopard, he was part of the metaphysics. Hemingway did not propose to explain that or a lot of other matters connected with the story. While he knew what they were, he was under no obligation to tell anyone about them.

Among the other matters that Hemingway felt no obligation to explain was the fact that Helen was a composite of at least two women. One, if we can trust the story, was the munificent lady in New York. The other was his own second wife, Pauline. He had seen her in action during the recent safari, and he could not forget that her father was among the wealthiest citizens of northeastern Arkansas or that her paternal uncle, Gustavus Adolphus Pfeiffer, was a millionaire who had generously underwritten the trip to Africa with a grant-in-aid of twenty-five thousand dollars. While Hemingway had not by any means surrendered his integrity as a writer in the presence of riches, and while he often complained at this period about his shrunken bank balance, he knew very well that among

There was a log house, chinked white with mortar, on a hill above the lake. There was a bell on a pole by the door to call the people in to meals. Behind the house were fields and behind the fields was the timber. . . . A road went up to the hills along the edge of the timber and along that road he picked blackberries. Then that log house was burned down and all the guns that had been on deer foot racks above the open fire place were burned and afterwards their barrels, with the lead melted in the magazines, and the stocks burned away, lay out on the heap of ashes that were used to make lye for the big iron soap kettles, and you asked Grandfather if you could have them to play with, and he said, no. You see they were his guns still and he never bought any others. Nor did he hunt any more. The house was rebuilt in the same place out of lumber now and painted white and from its porch you saw the poplars and the lake beyond; but there were never any more guns. The barrels of the guns that had hung on the deer feet on the wall of the log house lay out there on the heap of ashes and no one ever touched them.

his "defects" was a liking for the pleasures wealth could buy. The dying writer in his story was an image of himself as he might have been if the temptation to lead the life of the very rich had ever overcome his determination to continue his career as a writer.

A similar mixture of "true stuff" and invention appears in the stream-of-consciousness monologues which periodically interrupt the surface movement of the story. These represent Harry's memories of his past life, and many of them, naturally enough, are Hemingway's own. It is only by knowing the course of his life in some detail that one can sort out truth from fiction. As in any process of free association of ideas and scenes, the episodes Harry recalls ignore strict chronology. Yet if they are arranged in historical sequence, they provide a rough running account of scenes from the life of the author. The earliest of Harry's internal landscapes reveals "a log house, chinked white with mortar, on a hill above the lake." The lake is Walloon, nine miles from Petoskey, Michigan, where Hemingway spent the seventeen summers of his boyhood, beginning in 1900. The house is that of Grandpa Bacon, an aged patriarch with a red beard who was still alive when the Hemingway children were growing up. References to the First World War are brief. There is one to the fighting around Monte Corvo on the Italian-Austrian front, a passage at arms that Hemingway had heard of but not seen, and another about trench warfare, presumably in France, in which an officer named Williamson is disembowelled by a German stick-bomb in the tangled barbed wire of no man's land.

Hemingway returns to his own experience with a graphic cityscape—the hilltop on the Left Bank in Paris where he lived with his first wife, Hadley, in a walk-up flat in the rue du Cardinal Lemoine from the spring of 1922 until they left for Toronto in the summer of 1923. It is a part of Paris that has changed relatively little in forty-odd years, and although Hemingway undoubtedly invented touches here and there, the *quartier* is still recognizable from his description. The allusion to the *femme de ménage* and her views on the disadvantages of the eight-hour working day is

CONTINUED ON PAGE 90

On the morning of May 13, 1783, a group of officers of the Continental Army gathered at Verplanck House near the Hudson River village of Fishkill, New York. The house, built of stone in the Dutch style, was headquarters for General Friedrich Wilhelm von Steuben, the Prussian professional who had done so much to train and reorganize Washington's Revolutionary army. As the senior officer present, Baron von Steuben presided.

The meeting's moving force, however, was Major General Henry Knox, Chief of Artillery for the Continental Army. For some years Knox had been thinking about a ribbon that veterans might wear to show they had fought for the liberty of their nation. He envisaged a badge or memento that could be passed proudly from generation to generation.

Now Knox's dream was nearing fulfillment. In April he had sketched out an organization and made a rough draft of its rules; then he had checked his ideas with other officers of the Army, which was camped for the winter around Newburgh, New York. Encouraged by their reactions, he arranged for meetings in May to shape his proposed society. Now, at Verplanck

House, a charter was discussed and unanimously approved by all present. America's first veterans' group had been formed.

The Society of the Cincinnati, as the new organization was called, was not destined for obscurity. Before the end of the critical period between 1783 and 1790, it would touch off an international furor and shake the wobbly foundations of the new American republic. Along the way it would embarrass George Washington, distress John Adams, alarm Thomas Jefferson, amuse Benjamin Franklin, and in some way stir the lives of nearly all leading Americans.

None of the officers assembled at Verplanck House could foresee any of this, of course. They had more immediate concerns, and one was the disbanding of their army. Cornwallis had surrendered at Yorktown nearly two years before, and American ministers in Europe had been negotiating the peace settlement. With the day of separation coming on, Washington's officers wished simply to preserve the camaraderie established by the war and to help ensure that the ideals for which they had fought would be realized.

And there were other considerations. To put it baldly, many officers had financial worries. The Con-

A "New and

tinental Congress had been lax about its soldiers' pay, and the future for many was uncertain. Some, like George Washington, could rely on private resources; others were in straits. Von Steuben himself was a case in point. After the surrender at Yorktown, high-ranking officers of the American, French, and British forces competed at entertaining each other—except for von Steuben. He had already given up his watch to pay the doctor's bill of his aide-de-camp. Humiliated because he could not be even a moderate host, he tried selling his favorite horse. "We are, God knows, miserably poor," the Baron complained. "We are constantly feasted by the French without giving them even a bit of bratwurst." Telling his aide to "take my silver spoons and forks and sell them," he declared: "I will give one grand dinner to our allies, should I eat my soup with a wooden spoon forever after."

The engraving below, taken from a membership certificate of the Society of the Cincinnati, was designed by Major Pierre Charles L'Enfant. The primary features of its rousing iconography are an eagle of destruction and an armored America, sword upraised and foot crushing England's spear and shield, chasing away Britannia and her cowed lion.

Finding themselves in similar trouble, many officers were in a lean and dangerous mood. In the winter of 1782–83 they had circulated two "addresses" protesting the "coldness and severity" of their treatment by Congress. Mutiny had hovered over the Newburgh encampment, and Washington had been compelled to warn Congress that "the patriotism and long suffering of this army are well-nigh exhausted." In the end, only the General's powerful personality, together with an eloquent appeal to his men's sense of duty, had calmed the winds of discontent.

But the basic matter of money—and the inability or reluctance of Congress to provide it—remained. It was natural, then, for officers to band together to protect their common interests. If Congress had been remiss on salaries, it could now at least be gracious enough to provide pensions or other financial security for America's out-of-work soldiers. And what Congress did not provide could be made up by an organization that would help those in need.

Were social ties and mutual worries the only considerations at Verplanck House? It is impossible not to assign mundane motives to most of those present, but they were idealistic, too, and this came through at

"Strange Order of Men"

Just what moved those Revolutionary War officers to form the Society of the Cincinnati, America's first veterans' organization? Some said it was treason

By EDWIN A. HOEY

SOCIETY OF THE CINCINNATI

least in the name they chose for their new society.

In the fifth century B.C., Lucius Quinctius Cincinnatus left his farm to lead his fellow Romans in victorious battle against invading enemies. Then Cincinnatus set a precedent for future civilian-soldiers by rejecting the Senate's offer of civil power and returning to furrow and family. To men imbued with the neoclassic spirit of the late eighteenth century, Cincinnatus must have had a special appeal. The Revolutionary officers honored his name and example by calling their organization the Society of the Cincinnati.

In view of the simple virtues that the name implied, it is perhaps unfortunate that Henry Knox played an important role in drawing up the Cincinnati's charter. Timothy Pickering, Quartermaster General and himself a member of the society, would later remark that Knox's language "bore the marks of his pomposity." Even the charter's title had a solemn ring; it was called the "Institution."

Nevertheless, a true patriot could hardly quibble about the three principles—financial, fraternal, and patriotic—to which the society proposed to devote itself:

An incessant attention to preserve inviolate those exalted rights and liberties of human nature, for which they have fought and bled, and without which the high rank of a rational being is a curse instead of a blessing.

An unalterable determination to promote and cherish, between the respective States, that union and national honor, so essentially necessary to their happiness, and the future dignity of the American Empire.

To render permanent the cordial affection subsisting among the Officers. This spirit will dictate brotherly kindness in all things, and particularly extend to the most substantial acts of beneficence ... towards those Officers and their Families who unfortunately may be under the necessity of receiving it.

It was not these goals but the rules set up to carry them out that almost brought down the Cincinnati.

The General Society was divided into state societies, each completely autonomous, which collected funds from members and kept in touch with the others by circular letters and periodic general meetings. Membership was limited to those officers of the Army (later the Navy would be included) who had served to the end of the war, had resigned with honor after three years' service, or had been "deranged" (the term meant honorably retired) by act of Congress. When a charter member died, succession would pass to his "eldest male posterity" or to another branch of his family "who may be judged worthy." In other words, only one member of each family, usually the oldest son, could belong at any one time. To acknowledge America's debt to France, her ally in the Revolution, provision was made for a French society. The Cincin-

nati eventually decided to include all foreign officers who could meet the general requirements.

Recognizing that there were men other than officers who might be "eminent for their abilities and patriotism," the Institution set up honorary memberships. These were good only for the lifetime of the person concerned and could not be inherited.

Knox had dreamed of a distinguishing insignia for veterans, and the Institution provided for one. A medal, or badge, of gold would be struck. It would hang from a blue ribbon edged with white, thus uniting the colors of America and France. On one side the medal would show Cincinnatus being presented with a sword by three senators, his wife and plow waiting discreetly in the background. The other side would depict the farmer-hero being crowned with a wreath by Fame. Major Pierre Charles L'Enfant, lately of the Continental Corps of Engineers, won the commission to design the society's certificate of membership and badge. L'Enfant chose the American bald eagle for the basic design of the medal.

With the groundwork laid, the founders now needed a president general, as their leader was to be called. The choice was obvious: George Washington was unanimously elected at the Verplanck meeting. Generals Knox, von Steuben, and William Heath were asked to call on Washington and request his acceptance. They did so, and at Newburgh on May 20 the General agreed to serve.

Once the Commanding General had signed on, other officers were quick to follow. During the summer of 1783, societies were founded in all thirteen states, the original membership eventually totalling some 2,400 men out of the nearly 6,000 who were eligible. Among the joiners were such luminaries as Alexander Hamilton, Nathanael Greene, John Paul Jones, Thaddeus Kosciusko, Horatio Gates, James Monroe, William Moultrie, "Light-Horse Harry" Lee, "Mad" Anthony Wayne, and William Clark. The distinguished roster in itself aided recruitment. The order's reception in France was even more enthusiastic. Louis XVI relaxed a rule which forbade his officers to wear foreign decorations. Major L'Enfant, with forgivable partiality, observed that the badge had become more popular than the traditional Order of St. Louis. In all, 356 men, the cream of the *ancien régime,* joined the French society. Lafayette, de Grasse, and Rochambeau tried to outdo one another in the interest they could show. Denis-Jean Dubouchet, who had fought for America but not long enough to meet society requirements, crossed the Atlantic to plead his case. He succeeded, getting an appointment from Washington himself, and returned to France feeling well rewarded for his pains.

Unhappily for the order, such enthusiasm was not typical at home. Watchful eyes in America were viewing the fraternal developments with alarm. The opening salvo of criticism, fired in the autumn of 1783, was a fifteen-page pamphlet entitled *Considerations on the Order or Society of Cincinnati*. The author, deciding to counter one name from antiquity with another, had signed himself "Cassius"; his real name

tion of the Constitution and would attack idolatry of Washington as a first step toward monarchy. As self-appointed watchdog to keep "our liberties from being fooled away," he never hesitated to speak his mind.

On the title page of his pamphlet, Burke put the Biblical admonition "Blow ye the trumpet in Zion." And blow he did. He charged that the members of the Cincinnati had no intention of imitating the society's

Washington's Farewell to His Officers, *painted in 1865 by Alonzo Chappel, occurred in December of 1783, a few months after the Cincinnati was formed. The work affirms the war-born spirit of camaraderie that gave rise to the society.*

was Aedanus Burke, of South Carolina. Born in County Galway to a family accustomed to fighting British rule, Burke had come to America as a youth and then studied law. He served during the early part of the Revolution (not long enough to make him eligible for the Cincinnati) and later became a member of the bench of South Carolina. He helped form the state's democratic rules of government, rejoicing over the end of "unnatural distinctions of noblemen and commons." In later years, he would oppose ratifica-

namesake by returning to obscure citizenship. He predicted that they would develop a hereditary peerage, eventually seizing control of all civil and military offices and destroying all hope of putting democratic theory into practice. "The Order is planted in a fiery, hot ambition, and thirst for power," cried Burke, "and its branches will end in tyranny." Never one to understate an argument, he put the society's membership at 10,000, more than quadrupling its size. But his arguments, no matter how overblown, found a

47

ready audience. Cassius' ideas spread quickly and made the society, as Thomas Jefferson would wryly note, "the subject of general conversation."

Criticism crackled through the colonies. Northerner Elbridge Gerry and southerner James Madison both predicted that the society would be able to control elections. Fiery old Sam Adams accused it of being "as rapid a Strike towards an hereditary Military Nobility as was ever made in so short a time." A less prominent but pun-loving critic said in the *Virginia Gazette*, "I dislike [the society] more particularly for having two 'Cins' in it."

To some, the Institution raised a number of dangerous questions. Hadn't the war been fought partly to end such abuses of privilege as primogeniture? Why hadn't the officers made express provision to look after the army's rank and file? Why should honorary membership be limited to citizens "whose views may be directed to the same laudable objects with those of the Cincinnati"? Wasn't this an attempt to attract influential men with the carrot of membership? Finally, why was it suggested that letters circulated among state societies concern themselves not only with Cincinnati affairs but also with "the general union of the States"? Critics remembered how they themselves had used committees of correspondence to foment a revolution. And what about those French members? The Massachusetts legislature warned that they were "strongly attached to a government essentially different in principles from the republican constituents of the United States."

In money-conscious New England, the prospect of military influence in financial affairs touched off a display of Yankee fireworks. Some citizens stoutly defended the idea of government aid to officers. Others were vehemently opposed. Citizens using such pseudonyms as "An Officer," "An Impartial Farmer," "A Continentalist," and "Cives" had at each other in the press. Signing himself "Honorius," young Noah Webster took time off from his words to support government subsidies for Continental officers, but the town meeting of Killingworth, Connecticut, pointed out cantankerously that the first Cincinnatus had not felt compelled to retire on government funds. A statewide convention at Middletown—called expressly to consider the Cincinnati problem and keep watch on this "new and strange order of men"—commended Burke's pamphlet "to the notice and perusal of the people at large."

In Rhode Island things were not much better. Nathanael Greene, president of the state society, conceded that his order was "thought to contain dangerous designs, pregnant with mischief, and . . . ruinous to the people." In fact, rumor soon spread that Rhode

This dazzling jewel-studded version of the badge of the society was presented to Washington in 1784 by officers of the French navy; subsequent presidents general have worn it on occasions of high ceremony. The insignia's motto, which translates as "He left all to preserve the Republic," encircles the scene of Cincinnatus' being called to arms. This priceless badge contains 137 separate gems.

48

Island's legislature had disenfranchised society members and had banned them from "holding any post of honour and trust" in its government. Although archives of the state record no such law, the rumor was widely accepted as fact.

With matters at this pitch, controversy quickly leaped the Atlantic. The Comte de Mirabeau, a French nobleman who had turned against the old order and who later became a leader in the early stages of the French Revolution, showed his radical sympathies by translating the Cassius pamphlet into French, adding some jabs of his own. And liberal spirits in France and Germany, who had hailed America's victory as a blow for democratic principles, bemoaned what they considered an aristocratic aberration on the part of their heroes.

With Europe busily inspecting America's washline, three leading American diplomats abroad were quick to react, each in his own way. From Paris, John Jay commented sourly that if the society "took well in the states," he "would not care if the Revolutionary War had succeeded or not."

John Adams was at first only a lukewarm objector. Writing to Lafayette from Holland, he said he "disapproved . . . with as much tranquility and self-recollection, and phlegm, if you will, as I had been a native, full-blooded Dutchman." And he added that the order might be "the first step taken to deface the beauty of our temple of liberty." Later, Adams' mood went from phlegmatic to splenetic. Perhaps put out by the hostile treatment he received at London's aristocratic Court of St. James's, he wrote to Elbridge Gerry: "The Cincinnati is the deepest piece of cunning yet attempted. It is sowing the seeds of all that European courts wish to grow up among us, viz. of vanity, ambition, corruption, discord, and sedition."

The third diplomat was less angry than sardonically amused. Old Ben Franklin, another peace commissioner in Paris, just could not take the order with complete seriousness. As a scientist, he showed how the members' patriotic blood would be watered down from generation to generation. As a scholar, he criticized the Latin of the society's motto, *Omnia reliquit servare rempublicam.** As a naturalist, he regretted that the Cincinnati had chosen for its symbol the eagle, "a bird of bad moral character" and "a rank coward." Franklin commented that the founders of the society had been "too struck with the ribbands and crosses they have seen hanging in the button-holes of foreign officers," but he concluded that "if people can be pleased with small matters, it is a pity that they should not have them."

Like Franklin, even some of the pillars of the society were able to laugh off the criticism. While sending nervous notes to Washington, Henry Knox was writing to von Steuben:

Your Society, monsieur baron, has occasioned great jealousies among the good people of New England, who say it is altogether an outlandish creature, formed by a foreign allegiance.... You see how much you have to answer for by the introduction of your European distinctions.

Von Steuben parodied Cassius in his even jollier reply:

A ça, Monsieur le Cincinnatus! your pernicious designs are then unveiled. You wish to introduce dukes and peers into our republic? No, my lord; no, your Grace, that will not do; there is a Cassius more far-sighted than this German baron: . . . When I shall tell him that the young Marquis Henry Knox is already promised in marriage to a Princess Hyder Ali . . . and that the King of Spain wishes to accept the place of Treasurer of the Order, then, Blow Ye the Trumpet in Zion!

At Mount Vernon, however, the society's president general was not in a bantering mood. Seeking peace, Washington had found a furor. He had not formed the Cincinnati and had not asked to become its leader. He had come home to Virginia in hopes, as he wrote to Lafayette, of "retiring within myself . . . envious of none . . . determined to be pleased with all." But Henry Knox was writing him to report that the waves of hostility were sweeping New England, and that the Massachusetts society had not dared to call more attention to itself by appointing honorary members.

Always concerned about his "public image," as a later age would call it, Washington was highly embarrassed by the general outcry. What reflected on the society, he thought, reflected on him. He was also deeply worried about his nation, which was in danger of flying apart in the loose straps of confederation. He realized that a public battle over the society was just what the country did not need.

Thomas Jefferson, always anxious to lay an "axe to the root of pseudo-aristocracy," did nothing to ease Washington's worries. He was all for having members of the society "distribute their funds, renounce their existence," and "melt up their eagles." He urged that Washington stand "on ground separated" from the order so that "the head of our revolution may in no

CONTINUED ON PAGE 72

* The motto, a reference to Cincinnatus, may be translated into modern idiom as "He dropped everything to save the nation." The motto's author has never been established, but whoever it was gave Latin buffs something to chew on. Since the motto expressed purpose, it more correctly should have used the imperfect subjunctive, *Omnia reliquit ut servaret rempublicam.* L'Enfant also added to the confusion. His sketch for the design of the badge showed *Omnia relinquit servare rempublican,* adding an "n" to the second word. This spelling was used on the certificate but not on the eagle badge itself, which somehow came out with *Omnia relinqt servat rempb.* Valuing tradition over the niceties of syntax, the Cincinnati has left everything the way it originally appeared.

49

UNCLE TOM?
NOT BOOKER T.

By JACQUELINE JAMES

In 1901 when Booker Taliaferro Washington's memoir *Up From Slavery* was published, William Dean Howells called him "a public man second to no other American in importance." He was also a very private man. His life was far more complicated than the readers of his most famous book could imagine—then or even today, sixty-seven years afterward. Almost hidden within his vast correspondence is the evidence that the soft-spoken man who won such public recognition as an educator was actually waging a secret fight for the Negro's civil rights. Politically, he managed to do more and do it earlier than the militants of his day who scornfully dismissed him as an Uncle Tom.

Eighteen months before the publication of Washington's autobiography, Howells had seen the public man impressively honored. On the night of December 4, 1899, Howells had put on full evening dress and gone to the Madison Square Garden Concert Hall in New York to a fund-raising meeting for Booker Washington's school, Tuskegee Institute in Tuskegee, Alabama. Howells represented literary New England in a gathering that drew not only editors, ministers, and descendants of early abolitionists, but New York's oldest society and America's newest wealth. Men such as August Belmont, William Dodge, Jacob Schiff, Collis Huntington, John D. Rockefeller, and J. P. Morgan crowded the hall, and the presiding speaker of the evening was ex-Senator and former Secretary of the Interior Carl Schurz.

Although the list of box holders was a fund raiser's dream, no one was so crude as to pass a tall silk hat that night. William H. Baldwin, president of the Long Island Railroad and treasurer of Tuskegee's board of trustees, asked the audience to go home and consider what they had heard. He gave the facts and figures of the achievement that had brought such a luminous assemblage to hear a speech by a former slave. Eighteen years before, the Alabama legislature had appropriated $2,000 to pay teachers' salaries in a non-existent normal school for Negroes. When a young mulatto named Booker Washington was appointed to manage this ironic appropriation, he pledged his own salary to buy an abandoned plantation called the Old Burnt Place and started the school with seventeen students. Now, Baldwin told his audience, Dr. Washington (who had subsequently been awarded an honorary degree by Harvard) was educating 1,200 Negro boys and girls in forty-two buildings on more than 2,000 acres of land. The institution by then was worth $300,000.

Washington had seen to it that students built those buildings, paying for their education and learning a trade as they did so. He had raised the money—dollar by dollar—to expand and run a school which now needed nearly $65,000 a year just to keep going. The

This picture of President Theodore Roosevelt's visit in 1905 to Washington's school—Tuskegee Institute in Alabama—symbolizes the former slave's incredible achievement. The student guard in the foreground was not merely ceremonial; the President's Negro policy enraged many white southerners.

51

state of Alabama had been more than willing to let him do all the work. Its yearly appropriation by 1899 was $4,500, and Washington had to ask northern philanthropists to donate the rest of the operating expenses. Now he was asking for an endowment fund of a million dollars. Former President Grover Cleveland, who had planned to preside at the Madison Square fund-raising meeting, sent a letter when illness prevented his coming—and a promise of $25,000 from an anonymous donor in the Middle West.

Yet the chief drawing card of the evening—the reason for standees in the packed concert hall—was Booker Washington, public speaker. He was not only an earnest Negro educator, a self-made man who answered all the popular requirements; he was also a great orator. As Howells later recalled:

I heard Mr. Washington speak at a meeting which had been addressed by several distinguished white speakers. When this marvelous yellow man came upon the platform and stood for a moment, with his hands in his pockets, and with downcast eyes and then began to *talk* at his hearers, the clearest, soundest sense, he made me forget all those distinguished white speakers. . . . It was somewhat the manner of [Othello] when he defends himself to the Venetian Senate.

Common sense, Howells thought, was the dominant mood of *Up From Slavery*. "He has lived heroic poetry and he can, therefore, afford to talk simple prose. Simple prose it is, but of sterling worth." Readers in 1901 thought so—and so did successive generations. In the sixty-seven years since its publication it has become a recognized American classic and is available in five different editions. This was not Washington's intention when he wrote his book. He was a man of action and never considered himself a writer. He took time out from the consuming job of raising funds for Tuskegee to tell his own story because he had been persuaded that it would bring in money for the school, which indeed it did. Andrew Carnegie, who met the endowment goal almost singlehanded three years after the Madison Square meeting, was relatively unim-

pressed by Washington until he read *Up From Slavery*.

It is hard to imagine how the book could have been more successful. Yet anyone who knows what the author left out cannot help realizing that it could certainly have been more candid. If Washington had told the whole story it would have been obvious that he was not solely an educator. And William Dean Howells could hardly have said, "By precept and by practice he counsels . . . a manly fortitude in bearing the wrongs that cannot now be righted and a patient faith in the final kindliness and ultimate justice of the Anglo-Americans. His counsel has been for the Afro-American to forego politics, at least for the present."

Washington indeed saw nothing to be gained by an open fight over the Negro's rights in 1900. The crucial word here is "open." Washington believed in fighting —and, if possible, in winning. By 1900 he had already begun a secret battle to keep southern legislatures from denying the Negro the franchise. Howells' embarrassing praise—one of the many remarks that later helped give Washington a reputation as an Uncle Tom—was one of the crosses he had to bear. He was acutely sensitive to criticism as a leader, but he cared most deeply about results. He let everyone see his main concern— the long-range program of educating the Negro for responsible citizenship. He felt that he could not let the readers of *Up From Slavery* see his hopes for the Negro's final complete integration into American life —or his own more immediate fight for political justice —without endangering both prospects.

The "Negro problem," as far as the audience gathered at Madison Square was concerned, was solely the result of the black man's own illiteracy, immorality, and sloth, and Washington was going to solve it. Speaker after speaker assured possible patrons that their consciences could be cleared by giving money to Tuskegee. "There is no longer the old problem of what to do with the Negro," said William Baldwin. "That question has been settled. The problem now is one of

The tilted, seedy building above was the home of Washington's grim-looking owners, James and Elizabeth Burroughs. As a child, Booker called it the "Big House."

co-operation and help and work." Baldwin was an unusual philanthropist, but he shared the belief of most white Americans, as the new century began, that the passage of time meant inevitable progress.

It was not, however, a time of progress for the American Negro. In the grim nineties, when there were more lynchings than at any other time in American history, the South, with the connivance of a largely indifferent North, was rapidly taking away all the rights given the freedman during Reconstruction. In 1900 the educated Negro minority could not help but see its problem as primarily a political one. In the South, state after state was rewriting its Reconstruction constitution to disfranchise, by one device or another, its colored voters—who were thereby doomed to political impotence for the next fifty years. Mississippi had begun it in 1890, followed by South Carolina in 1895 and Louisiana in 1898. When Washington wrote *Up From Slavery,* he knew that Virginia and Alabama had constitutional conventions coming up in 1901.

At this critical time for the Negro, Washington's position was unique. He was an ambassador—very much without portfolio and with little leverage—from a small, diffuse country-within-a-country. He was the one man whom the majority of both races trusted. From this perilous summit he was expected to protect the Negroes in the South and protest with those of the North, to rally the silent white southern moderates, and to stem the power of the racists as best he could—and in the North to get contributions from both white liberals and conservative businessmen for his school. He managed to do more of these things at once than anyone realized because inevitably some of his alignments were private. William E. B. DuBois, Washington's chief antagonist in later years, said in his review of *Up From Slavery:* "It is no ordinary tribute to this man's tact and power that, steering as he must amid so many diverse interests and opinions, he today commands not simply the applause of those who believe in his theories, but also the respect of those who do not."

The editors of the intellectual weekly the *Outlook,* who serialized *Up From Slavery* before it was published in book form, wanted Washington to comment more on the stormy contemporary racial scene. He refused. He was writing a personal, not a political, book. Reviewers inevitably noticed the omission, but as the *Nation's* critic said, "It is not as if Mr. Washington had not written elsewhere of Negro lynching and disfranchisement."

He had done so in a successful little book called *The Future of the American Negro,* published shortly before the Madison Square fund-raising meeting. (It was one of the unforeseen consequences of *Up From Slavery's* overwhelming popularity that so many readers in the future would never know that Washington had written anything else.) Washington included in this earlier book the substance of two open letters he had written—a strong protest against lynching, which he managed to have printed in every possible southern newspaper in the summer of 1899; and an earlier letter to the Louisiana constitutional convention, which had met in 1898 to consider how to keep Negroes from voting without actually saying so.

"I entreat you," Washington wrote the Louisiana lawmakers, "not to pass such a law that will prove an eternal millstone about the neck of your children." In *Up From Slavery* he wrote one strong prophetic paragraph. Unless literacy tests, or any other changes in the franchise, were applied "without double dealing or evasion to both races alike . . . [it] will be, like slavery, a sin that at some time we shall have to pay for." He made no public comment then on the device the Louisiana convention had, in spite of his letter, finally chosen—the so-called "grandfather clause," which could not possibly be administered fairly to both races. In effect, the clause restricted the privilege of voting to all whose grandfathers had enjoyed it; this included nearly all white men, even illiterates. But for Negroes, most of whose grandparents had been slaves, it was virtual disfranchisement.

There is a story behind the conclusion of *Up From Slavery* that shows clearly what Booker Washington thought—and did—about the grandfather clause. The way he wrote that conclusion illustrates, as nothing else can, the different levels of his life at that critical moment: "As I write the closing words of this autobiography I find myself—not by design—in the city of Richmond, Virginia . . . where, about twenty-five years ago, because of my poverty I slept night after night under the sidewalk." He had been asked to speak, he went on, before an integrated audience in a hall which Negroes had never before been allowed to use. "In the presence of hundreds of coloured people, many distinguished white citizens, the City Council, the State legislature and state officials, I delivered my message, which was one of hope and cheer; and from the bottom of my heart I thanked both races for this welcome back to the state that gave me birth."

On a personal level, Washington's conclusion was certainly sincere. He was moved by the occasion and by the public *rapprochement* between the races which he had brought about. However, he never mentioned what actually brought him to Richmond. The aesthetics of the book would have made a recital of the facts inappropriate, but more important, the whole truth would have been politically indiscreet.

The facts were that the man who urged Washington to come to Richmond was a Negro lawyer named Giles Jackson—and Negro lawyers were at that time usually regarded as either ludicrous or suspect. Jackson was neither. He was a city leader and vice president of the National Negro Business League (founded by Booker Washington the year before), whose local chapter had issued the formal invitation. Giles Jackson was also a link between Washington and the white moderates in the city of Richmond, who had good reason to respect the Negro community. Not long before, when the city had needed money to keep the schools open, no white bank had been able to lend them fifty thousand dollars, but a Negro bank had been able and willing to lend them double the amount.

One provision of Virginia's proposed constitution divided money to schools by race—white tax money to support white schools, Negro taxes to support Negro ones. This would obviously result in Negro schools getting less per pupil than white schools and considerably less than they had been getting. White leaders with troubled consciences urged Jackson to get Booker Washington to come to speak out on this; there was a chance he might have some influence. But as for the primary purpose of the new constitution, the disfranchisement of the Negro by a grandfather clause or some other such device, Jackson wrote Washington confidentially that neither he nor anyone else could stop it: "This they will do at all hazards."

Washington had no reason to doubt it. The Louisiana legislature had paid little attention either to Washington's open letter of 1898 and the editorial support it got in the South, or to their own United States senators, both of whom had publicly stated that the grandfather clause was obviously unconstitutional. But no test case had yet reached the Supreme Court. Since 1899 Washington had been the leader of a small group of Negroes who were raising money to finance such a court test. Jackson, in urging Washington to speak in Richmond on the school issue, promised him that a large share of the proceeds from his speech would be donated to his anti-grandfather-clause fund. As a result, the distinguished audience, including the Virginia legislature, unwittingly helped contribute one hundred dollars to a fund designed to disallow its own proposed disfranchisement legislation.

From 1901 on, Booker Washington's political involvements became more important, and secrecy was therefore even more essential. For in 1901, Theodore Roosevelt became President. Within hours after he was sworn in, he was writing to Booker Washington, ". . . I must see you as soon as possible." Washington's new role as arbiter of all Roosevelt's Negro appointments and even of some southern white ones (a role carried on under Taft as well, although with diminished influence) had constantly to be concealed from a hostile Democratic press.

It was also in 1901 that Washington's home state of Alabama rewrote its constitution, complete with a grandfather clause and, as one delegate said with satisfaction, "enough traps to catch every Negro in Africa." Washington, who had lobbied against it with every subtle maneuver he could devise, undertook secretly to challenge it in the Supreme Court almost as soon as it was ratified. The case was eventually lost, but it was the first of a series of landmark cases that Booker Washington initiated. That southern white moderates sometimes helped him in these litigations was kept so secret that often even in his private correspondence he used assumed names. If he had worked openly in these legal fights—against disfranchisement, segregation, and peonage, and on behalf of the rights of Negroes to sit on juries—he would have been run out of the South.

For Washington to make an effective fund-raising document out of his memoirs at a time when Negro abrasiveness or protest would automatically have scared off most of the country's potential donors required concealing some of the facts. His nine formative years as a slave had trained him well for this task. For small Booker had been born into a kind of vast secret society where conscious concealment was practiced every day. In *Up From Slavery* he not only presented a selective picture of his adult life; he also edited his childhood. The account of his early years was as much art as fact. Only a few people knew the truth. One of these was a mulatto relative named Biah Ferguson, and she put it succinctly: "He said a lot of things that weren't so and left out a lot that was."

Undoubtedly some of the inaccuracy in *Up From Slavery* was quite unintentional—the hurried recollection of a busy man who did not take time to look up old records and simply got mixed up on his own chronology, as most people do. Some of it was the dramatic exaggeration of a fluent speaker trying to make a point. And if in his memoir he could make comments about slavery in general through himself, he did so—even though specific facts might not have strictly applied to his own life.

However, other facts were clearly omitted by editorial choice. There had been an earlier version of his memoirs—a book called *The Story of My Life and Work*—consisting mainly of press clippings strung together by a narrative that was partly ghostwritten. It was published by a midwestern firm which sold its books by subscription only, primarily to Negroes, but Washington's white patrons saw it and Lyman Abbott,

TEXT CONTINUED ON PAGE 95

Tuskegee: Washington's Monument

The Lincoln Gate, above, had just been completed by its student builders when Frances Benjamin Johnston came to Tuskegee in 1902 to make a photographic record of Booker T. Washington's famous school. The institute, just twenty-one years old, had reached an impressive majority. Already, hundreds of its alumni were proving throughout the South what Washington believed—that the educated Negro could function with energy and self-reliance, even in the white man's world. Miss Johnston was a well-known photographer and was singularly suited for this assignment. A meticulous craftsman, she was also, apparently, fearless. She previously had covered accidents and had descended into mines to get pictures, and while she was on the Tuskegee assignment, shots were fired at her Negro guide. Miss Johnston's reaction was one of indignation, and she resolved to see that the sniper was punished. That "[she] will succeed I have no doubt," Booker Washington's secretary reported to him. The calm, composed pictures she took at Tuskegee have been called misleading, for while she was there the campus was in more than its usual flurry of building. Students were working on eleven new structures, and she must have shot her pictures carefully to exclude the piles of lumber and brick that dotted the school grounds. The tidy busyness that she recorded, however, was altogether typical. On the next eight pages, AMERICAN HERITAGE reproduces a group of her memorable photographs, taken from the extensive Johnston collection now housed in the Library of Congress.

In spite of an enormous demand, Tuskegee did not train domestics. The women at left were learning practical laundering methods so they could teach cleanliness to Negroes in their home communities. This picture was shot at Mount Meigs Institute, one of Tuskegee's offshoot schools. There were sixteen such schools operating by 1903.

Careful cultivation was essential in Tuskegee's poor, worn-out soil, according to George Washington Carver, who ran the department of agriculture. Both blacks and whites learned from his research. Tuskegee students put up many of the school's buildings, and in the process (below) they earned a valuable trade and also earned their board.

Tuskegee students would be in demand, Washington promised, because they would be trained "to do that which the world wants done." However whites might interpret this, he meant that alumnae trained in mattress making and basket weaving would teach these viable skills to other Negroes.

A white educator who inspected Tuskegee in 1903 stated: "The industrial work [is] the best I have ever seen." Along with manual trades such as shoemaking, students learned sophisticated mechanical skills. In 1898 they had wired their chapel—the first building in the county to be electrified.

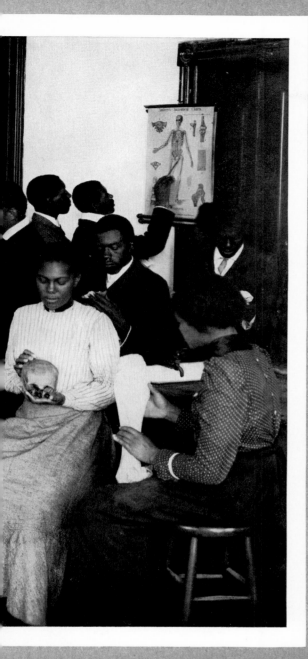

Although the struggling school needed the food and buildings provided by its agricultural and industrial programs, academic studies were still important, even in Tuskegee's earliest, leanest days. Andrew Carnegie gave money for the library (left) in 1901, and was so pleased by the results that two years later he gave $600,000 more. Physiology (above) was a sophomore subject. Teacher training (top right) was a favorite among the girls. American history (center right) was required in the first year, and seniors studied chemistry in the school's excellent laboratory. Graduates were encouraged to work toward educating the Negro race. Back in their own localities, many alumni helped build new schools and then taught in them.

This charming scene of Victorian repose illustrates Booker Washington's insistence on absolute cleanliness and genteel decorum. His students twitted him for his "gospel of the toothbrush," but he was determined that Tuskegee men and women should serve to dispel the myth of the dirty, shiftless Negro.

The kidnapped frontier woman might have thought twice about trying to escape had she known that what lay beyond—the way home—could be as dangerous as the Shawnees who held her

An Indian Captivity

By GARY JENNINGS

July 30, 1755, dawned clear and bright in Draper's Meadows, a tiny log-cabin community in what one day would be Blacksburg, Virginia. Soon most of the settlement's men and women were working in the scattered wheat and maize fields or expanding the unforested glades to increase their tillable land. One of the few to stay indoors was Mary Ingles, a raven-haired, blue-eyed matron who at twenty-three had already known an eventful life.

Her name had been Mary Draper when, in 1748, she first entered the New River valley. She came with her widowed mother and her brother, John, together with Thomas Ingles, his three sons, and a handful of pioneers enticed by the Loyal Land Company.

Draper's Meadows was the first organized English settlement that far west in the Allegheny Mountains, and Mary especially, of all its inhabitants, had several "firsts" to her credit. In 1750 she had accepted the proposal of one of Thomas Ingles' sons, William, and become the first English bride in that part of the mountains. A year later the couple's first son, Thomas, arrived—the first white child to be born on that frontier.

And now, on this summer's day, Mary and her

ILLUSTRATED BY DORIS JACKSON

George Caleb Bingham's Captured by Indians, *painted about 1848, might have been inspired by Mary Ingles' story.*

mother were keeping an eye on two-month-old George and hoping that little Tom wasn't getting into mischief outside. He wasn't, but others were —a band of Shawnee warriors hungry for plunder and eager to prove their bravery by acquiring scalps. The settlers at Draper's Meadows had little reason to fear an attack. True, Indians of many tribes—Shawnees to the west, Cherokees to the southwest, Catawbas to the southeast, and various Souian clans in eastern Virginia—used the main trail that followed the New River westward through the mountains toward the Kanawha and Ohio rivers. But Virginia's treaties with the Iroquois Confederacy had generally spared the area from disturbance by the Indians to the north and south; and except for isolated incidents of pilferage and harassment, the western Indians had left the Meadows pretty much alone.

What these secluded pioneers did not yet know was that almost two weeks earlier General Edward Braddock's force of British regulars and Virginia militiamen had been disastrously beaten by the French and Indians at Fort Duquesne, some three hundred miles to the north. Perhaps it was that that put the Shawnees into a warlike frame of mind; perhaps it was merely their own unpredictable temperament. At any event, this particular Shawnee band, previously undetected, were now exploding from their forest camouflage.

It is moot how many of that day's atrocities Mary Ingles observed. Her mother was tomahawked. Her brother's wife, Betty, attempted to flee with her baby, but she was brought down by an Indian's bullet that shattered her arm. Betty's baby was seized by a Shawnee who swung it by its heels, pulverizing its head against a log wall. At another cabin, fiery old Colonel James Patton, one of the land company's magnates, attempted to defend himself with his sword. Against impossible odds, he dispatched two of the savages before a bullet got him. Elsewhere in the settlement Casper Barrier fell dead, James Cull was seriously wounded, and Henry Leonard was knocked senseless. Mary, clutching her sons, was seized but was unharmed. She, the two boys, and Betty Draper were flung onto settlers' horses and driven off.

Out in the fields Will Ingles paused from his labors when he saw smoke, from the area of the cabins, threading upward above the towering canopy of forest. Although unarmed, he ran homeward; so did the other men, but they must have known they were too late. Most of the cabins were already crackling boxes of flame.

By then the raiders and their prisoners were well away and travelling fast. The Indians paused briefly at the lonely hut of Phil Barger, an old hermit. Enraged to discover nothing worth stealing there, they hacked off the old man's white-bearded head and took it along with them. A little farther on their way, they dropped the grisly souvenir on the doorstep of a Mrs. Lybrook.

They pressed on at a pace that was brutally punishing to the wounded Betty Draper; Mary, riding alongside, supported her sister-in-law as best she could. Fortunately, Tom and his baby brother, riding in the clutch of a murderer, seemed to think the cavalcade a grand lark. Their exuberance looked like bravery to the Shawnees, who from then on treated the boys with primitive respect and kindness.

True to their traditional values, the Shawnees spared themselves no more than they did their mounts or their prisoners. There were only brief halts, to eat rations of leathery jerked venison or to drink from springs. Seeking to outdo one another in endurance, the braves somehow slept as they rode; the children napped leaning against them, and Betty was in a merciful half-coma. Only Mary dared not doze at all.

The party travelled down the New River some forty miles before crossing to its western bank. They left the New at its junction with the Bluestone and went up and over Flat Top Peak. Then they made a short cut around some unfavorable terrain and came again to the river, now broadened by the waters of many tributaries into the Kanawha River, not far from present-day Charleston, West Virginia.

They camped at the Kanawha near the mouth of Campbell's Creek to take advantage of an adjacent salt lick. The Shawnees put Mary to work helping them boil down brine. During these several days Mary found opportunities to bathe and poultice Betty's broken arm; Betty was well on her way to recovery by the time the Shawnees loaded the salt on their newly acquired pack animals.

They followed the Kanawha until it joined the Ohio at Point Pleasant, and thence pursued the Ohio westward to a point opposite the mouth of the Scioto. There, on the north bank of the Ohio, was their principal town—the site of today's Portsmouth, Ohio. On the Indians' efficient ferry rafts the whole company crossed the river and were received in Shawnee Town with bonfires, dancing, and banqueting.

Mary soon found herself inside a malodorous thatched building. Squaws stripped her and divided her clothes among themselves; they pinched and prodded her, giggling at the whiteness of her body. Reclad in buckskins, she was led out again for a humiliatingly intimate inspection by some of the men.

That none of the prisoners was tortured or killed bespeaks the casual and mercenary motives of these Shawnees, who had perpetrated the massacre more to gain booty and to display their courage than to start a blood feud. The young Indians recounted their heroic and profitable adventure; they proudly displayed the scalps they had taken, and were recognized as braves by their elders. The major items of plunder, such as horses or slaves, were community property of the whole tribe and were assigned for use at the discretion of the chiefs. Betty was sent to Chillicothe, an outlying Shawnee village. She went, wan and submissive, having cared about nothing since her baby's murder. Mary's boys were taken from her; the distraught mother bade them show the same courage that they had exhibited thus far.

For a while thereafter Mary merely existed, letting the days wash over her, doing what she was bidden, eating scraps of unappetizing food, and sleeping on the vermin-ridden pallet allotted to her.

Gradually she came alive again, realizing that survival depended upon her proficiency as a worker. She was an able seamstress, and her skill with herbs, displayed in caring for Betty's shattered arm, qualified her to minister similarly to the Indians. Clearly she was more valuable alive than dead.

She knew it was inconceivable that Will Ingles could ever track the party that had brought her to the mouth of the Scioto. The only hope for her return—

and, with luck, the return of her sons—was for Mary to escape and walk the uncountable miles home.

Mary Ingles discovered that hers was not the only white face in Shawnee Town. Occasional French traders and *coureurs de bois* came to bargain muskets and manufactured goods for the Indians' furs, but Mary doubtless realized that none would imperil his lucrative trade, much less his life, by helping a captive to escape.

There was also another white woman in the town. In traditional accounts she has been called only "the Dutch woman," and much speculation has arisen about her. It became popular belief that she was old, fat, phlegmatic, and bestialized from long captivity. She was also generally believed to have come from Pennsylvania. But a recently published history of Virginia's Montgomery County contends that the Shawnees, returning from Draper's Meadows, had in fact visited one more homestead on the New River. There, according to this version, the Indians bedevilled old Henry Bingamin and carried off his wife. The Bingamins were of German extraction, and the traditional accounts may have confused "Deutsch" with "Dutch." Since the Bingamins later settled in Pennsylvania, their name probably passed from memory—hence merely "the Dutch woman" and hence the mistaken assertion that Pennsylvania was the place of her abduction.

At any rate, about two months after she was brought to the Shawnee town, Mary and Mrs. Bingamin were compelled to accompany an Indian party on a trek to the tribe's chief source of salt—Big Bone Lick, some one hundred miles to the west and across the Ohio in what today is Boone County, Kentucky.

Big Bone was a sight to see, for although it was surrounded by an unwholesome swamp, the lick itself had been a gathering place for animals from time immemorial. (A decade later Colonel Thomas Bullitt and his company of explorers and surveyors are said to have used the tusks and vertebrae of mastodons for tent poles and for stools and benches.) And even in Mary's day herds of buffalo and elk were still beating paths to the site. Such trails, as potential avenues to freedom, did not escape Mary's notice.

In addition to their duties in the camp itself, she and Mrs. Bingamin customarily foraged on the borders of the swamp for wild grapes, berries, and nuts to augment their diet.

When Mary first proposed flight, the older woman tried to discourage her. But Mary's resolve was so great that one afternoon her fellow prisoner reluctantly agreed to accompany her.

Each of the women had secreted a blanket, and each possessed a dull tomahawk which the Indians allowed them to use in gathering firewood. Mary managed to trade hers to a Frenchman in exchange for a sharper one, but the women were far from able to provision themselves properly for a long trek.

On the day of their decision, the two put all possible distance between themselves and the Shawnee camp, taking pains, however, to double back from their true course to throw off possible pursuers. At sundown, they hid among leaves and branches, waiting fearfully for the search they were sure must follow. Search the Indians did, but probably thinking that the women had fallen prey to wild beasts, they soon gave up. At dawn the women crept from hiding, unaware that the Indians had abandoned thought of further pursuit. Regaining their track, they angled back to the edge of the Ohio River. It does not strain credulity to surmise that the two women were overseen by a guardian angel. Most of their route would be through country that had never felt the tread of a white foot, through forests that had been standing for untold centuries, through the haunts of beasts that had seldom seen an interloper. In that land and in those days, animate danger did not lurk; it leapt unafraid. And even though explorers and land promoters later admitted that this countryside teemed with wildcats, bears, cougars, and wild boars, traditional accounts maintain that Mary Draper Ingles and Mrs. Bingamin never encountered anything even as fearsome as a polecat. But they would find that not all the dangers in these forests were four-footed.

For Mary this was no unthinking plunge into the unknown. She knew well enough what a stupendous chunk of country lay between her and home. Had there been a string-straight path from Big Bone Lick to Draper's Meadows, with not a single hill along the way, it would have measured two hundred and eighty miles. No one will ever know the exact length of the tortuous, up-and-down path the women had to travel —but it was close to eight hundred miles.

Their only certain pointer to the east and civilization was the Ohio River. Their starting point, on that morning after the escape, was some forty miles downstream and across the river from the bend that would someday sprout the city of Cincinnati. They trudged eastward, and for the first week or so the trip was almost pleasurable. It was the end of September, and the days seemed to take warmth from the flaming autumn foliage; the women averaged thirty miles a day. If their diet of pohickory nuts, chinquapins, papaws, and scuppernongs got monotonous, at least there was a sufficiency of it. The nights were getting crisper, but by burrowing deep into great banks of dead leaves and huddling together under their blankets, they slept without too much discomfort.

The only habitations they passed were a few beaver houses half-submerged in small wayside streams. But their trek was taking them through the squares and along the streets of many a city-to-be. Between Big Bone Lick and their first landmark —Shawnee Town, on the other side of the river—they wended through the future Kentucky market towns of Covington, Newport, Augusta, Maysville, and Vanceburg. They would have tried to add meat to their vegetarian menu, but their only weapon was one tomahawk—Mrs. Bingamin had either lost hers or got tired of carrying it —and Mary had scant idea how to use the thing for hunting game.

When the travellers came abreast of Shawnee Town they made a cautious detour inland. It added several miles to their trek but brought them good fortune. At dusk, they found a falling-down, deserted cabin. Beside it was a strangled patch of corn in the midst of which was a swaybacked old horse wearing a bell. They slept in the cabin and breakfasted on ears of raw corn, a welcome change from their accustomed diet.

When they moved on they took the horse. He was a wretchedly woebegone old skate that should have been riding, not ridden. But he was a source of encouragement for the women, who took turns riding and walking. Thus they passed the sites of present-day Ashland and Catlettsburg and came to the Big Sandy River where it debouches into the Ohio from the south. They found it uncrossable. Neither could swim, and they despaired of ever constructing a serviceable raft. They had to turn southward along the Big Sandy until it was shallow enough to ford. This took them more than twenty miles off course, to the Y where the Big Sandy is formed by the confluence of the Tug and Levisa forks. So much driftwood had piled up at the junction that it formed an unbroken but shifty bridge from one side to the other. After some hesitation, the women decided to brave it. They tried to get the horse over, too.

The women had to clamber precariously from tree trunk to stump to taproot as the mass of flotsam turned, skidded, or floated away beneath their weight. Halfway across, the melancholy old plug plunged through a drift and was stranded, bellied over a thick bole. The women tried heroically to free him, but they were helpless without a hoist of some sort. Finally they had to leave the poor nag marooned. They hurried on without looking back, and he let them depart without audible reproach.

After crossing the Big Sandy the two women found the going no longer easy or rapid. With October came colder weather. Their clothes were now tattered and their moccasins worn out. Even at night, curled up under shelving rocks, the women suffered greatly from exposure. Rains severely cut their fare, too. The trees and bushes were fast losing their fruit; nuts and berries fell and rotted on the ground. Often their only meal of the day was pieces of soft bark, roots, or any other edible-looking flora. Getting nearer to Mary's home—by imperceptible stages, but getting there—she and Mrs. Bingamin began to speculate on which of them would be driven to eat the other. They even drew lots. When Mary lost, she tried to insure that the grisly jest not become serious. She regaled her companion with tales of Will Ingles' wealth and of the reward he would pay the older woman for helping Mary get home. Mrs. Bingamin was larger and stronger than Mary, but the younger woman managed to placate her and still her tirade against having been inveigled into leaving the Shawnees to starve in the wilderness. Mary, too, was disheartened at the number of times they had to backtrack along an intervening stream before being able to cross it, and then having to come back all that way without having made a mile of homeward progress.

The success that the frontierswomen enjoyed in this heartbreaking trek was less mysterious to them than to anyone today who retraces their line of march. More than luck and guardian angels led Mary and Mrs. Bingamin to their primary goal, the Kanawha River, which they could follow to the New River and the home valley: the Indian paths, or traces, through the forest primeval were evident to them. A number of streams might be confusingly similar to the one they sought, but the great east-west road paralleled only the Kanawha. It must have been thus that the women found the river.

They passed the site of today's city of Huntington, detoured around the Guyandot River, forged northward through West Virginia's present Cabell and Mason counties, and then, where Point Pleasant now stands, came to the mouth of the Kanawha. Mary rejoiced as they turned along its western bank and headed directly south toward her beloved Meadows.

But there was as much cause for despair as rejoicing. Their journey was only half over; the mountains lay ahead; and the pilgrims were in sad shape. The weather was becoming increasingly bitter. In the foothills of the Alleghenies the women were blasted by icy winds sweeping down from the peaks. They bound shreds of their clothing around their feet with strands of the leatherwood shrub. This left them garbed only in their stolen blankets, now nearly threadbare. Food was just about nonexistent. Often, in desperation, they would seize and devour anything that was green and growing. As often as not this avidity would leave them doubled up with agonizing cramps or limp from vomiting or diarrhea. But even at such times, despite her pain or weakness, Mrs. Bingamin was still able to find strength to blame Mary and revile her with frightening malevolence.

They had only one filling meal during the whole time they struggled along the Kanawha. It is nauseating to contemplate, even from a distance of two centuries. Accounts vary as to whether it was a deer's head they found caught in driftwood or whether it was a raccoon. All agree, however, that it was in an advanced state of decomposition. Its fetid odor sickened the women even as they tore into it. But eat it they did, ravenously, and they carried the few remaining scraps of meat with them when they went on.

They groped along the Kanawha to Coal River, far up that stream, across it, back down again to the Kanawha, and on past the future site of Charleston. Daily they saw deer and other game foraging, but there was no way to run them down. Mary's tomahawk was also lost by now. Mrs. Bingamin was getting more rabid by the mile, her rage against her companion increasing with her pangs of hunger. Mary had grown

used to privation and the natural hazards they encountered; but the older woman's mounting madness was no natural thing, and Mary knew no defense.

They came at last to the salt lick near Campbell's Creek where Mary's party had camped on the way out. From here the journey became a nightmarish treadmill. Every league of the leafless forest was exactly like the one they had just covered. They crossed an interminable series of creeks, then unknown and unnamed —Rush, Pens, Fields, Slaughters, Kellys, Paint—each seemingly just like all the others.

When they worked their painful way around the falls of the Kanawha, the monotony of the country changed—for the worse. They were in regions that Mary had not seen with the Shawnees, because their overland short cut on the way out had bypassed this long loop of the river. Mary soon discovered that the Indians had had good reason to steer clear of the water route. For the two women had passed from the Kanawha valley into the awesome New River Gorge, which is said to be the only eastern rival of the Grand Canyon. For miles the river rampages like a millrace between grim rock cliffs and precipitous mountains that tower a thousand feet above the water. An experienced team of well-fed, well-equipped mountaineers would find the gorge an estimable test of skill and strength, even in the best of weather. The two emaciated women clutched at their flimsy blankets and bucked into the canyon against a fanged November gale.

The gorge has landmarks now—Penitentiary Rocks, Pope's Nose, Lovers' Leap, Hawk's Nest, War Ridge, Castle Rock, Stretcher's Neck. To the wretched women every one of these, whatever it might be called by a later generation, was an inimical, appalling barrier.

They fought against brush and vines that choked the canyon bottom; briars clawed through their blankets, and rocks shredded the rags wrapped around their feet. They scrabbled over boulders that had toppled down from the cliffs. They crept gingerly across talus slopes of avalanche debris. They wriggled under fallen trees and over slippery mudbanks. Often the riverbank would become a solid crag before them; the only way around was to wade out waist-deep into the blood-freezing cold of the river itself.

Somehow they made it through the gorge. They inched around the menacing butte of Flat Top Peak near the present town of Hinton to find that the going was easier, even though they were now impeded by the wide mouth of the Bluestone River. As they had done so often before, they turned upstream along the Bluestone until they could ford, and came back down it to the New again. The worst was over now, had they but known it. On this bank of the river it was a difficult way, but not an impossible one, to Draper's Meadows. But if Mary had met and surmounted all that nature had thrown at her, she had yet to confront one of the most frightening dangers of all.

They were about opposite the mouth of the East River, not more than forty-five miles in a straight line from home. It was twilight. Suddenly, according to the Ingles family account, the hunger-maddened Mrs. Bingamin leapt on the tired and unsuspecting Mary. So near collapse were both women that even this feeble tussle could have resulted in the death of one or both of them.

Horrified, Mary fought back. The woman's hands were around her as they grappled on the frozen ground. Mary finally wrenched free, and then fled—running, falling, running again—into a wilderness that was now less cruel than her erstwhile companion.

When she could run no more, Mary lay gasping in the shelter of a birch copse, praying that the gathering darkness would conceal her. "The Dutch woman" lurched past, fearfully close to Mary's hiding place. But eventually the sounds of her pursuit faded away down the riverside.

Mary stayed where she was until the moon rose. She had no choice but to continue upriver in the direction Mrs. Bingamin must have taken; so she went cautiously, stopping often to listen. And Mary's luck seemed to turn again: half hidden, half submerged under the riverbank lay an abandoned bark canoe.

She frenziedly bailed it out with cupped hands, unmindful as they turned blue and rigid with cold. The canoe was weatherbeaten and waterlogged, and Mary had never handled one. Nevertheless, with only a piece of driftwood for a paddle, she launched her leaky craft. Fortunately the water was low and her strength sufficient to reach the eastern bank.

Still, it seemed, good fortune was with her. Not far from her landing, Mary found a tumble-down log cabin, probably some trapper's summer camp. Protected from the elements, she dropped gratefully to its earthen floor, and slept. In the cold, gray overcast of morning, she found a patch of ground that had once

been a garden. Anxiously she searched every inch of it, and made her breakfast of two small, gnarled turnips.

Resuming her journey, she was startled to hear someone hailing her. It was Mrs. Bingamin, calling frantically from the opposite bank, begging her to come back and promising to behave. Disregarding the pleas for forgiveness and help, Mary maintained her pace. Even if she could trust the woman, she could not trust the canoe again, and there was no other way of getting across. Fortunately for Mary's peace of mind, Mrs. Bingamin eventually had to detour inland around a riverside marsh, out of sight and hearing.

But Mary soon had other worries. The canoe had delivered her from one predicament into another. Except for the menace of Mrs. Bingamin, the lay of the land on the other side of the river made for much easier going. Here on Mary's side, where the New River hugged the rugged base of Wolf Mountain, was the worst terrain she had yet encountered.

To traverse the mountainside she had to make her way through miles of rhododendron thickets called "laurel hells." Then there was Wolf Creek, covered with skim ice, through which she made a hesitant passage. Beyond was another mountain to whose subsequent appellation, "Angel's Rest," Mary doubtless would have taken strong exception. After fording more ice-rimmed water at Stony Creek, she saw before her Salt Pond Mountain. Here, in the late November snow, she edged her way for two miles around the fringe of almost perpendicular cliffs that abut the riverside. Just before sunset several days later, having met seemingly interminable new barriers, each more formidable than the last, Mary came to what most would have considered a dead end. It was Anvil Rock.

In the last light of day the limestone of this 280-foot cliff gleamed eerily and appeared to be devoid of footholds or ledges. As a final discouragement to a climber, it leans outward from the vertical, arching up to an overhanging crown.

Hopeful of wading in the river around the cliff's base, Mary tested the depth of the water, but she found that she could not plumb it. The waters swirled crazily in uncertain whirlpools. Overcome by weariness, dampness, and cold, Mary searched in despair for a sheltered spot to rest for the night. She found no cave, no hollow log, no bower of limbs and leaves. After having come so far, tantalizingly near home, she appeared doomed to end her journey and her life in the snow at the foot of Anvil Rock.

In the morning she rose stiff, swollen, and sore. As much from desperation as from hope, she scanned Anvil Rock again, knowing that to climb around and over it was her only chance. Since morning shadows

Mr. Jennings is a free-lance writer living in New York. AMERICAN HERITAGE is grateful to George Green Shackelford, professor of history at Virginia Polytechnic Institute at Blacksburg, for his valuable research and editorial contributions in the preparation of this article.

reveal the perspectives indicative of ledges which are concealed by the shimmering rays of the setting sun, Mary Draper Ingles found a devious way to ascend what had appeared to be an unscalable cliff. It was now only another mountain, albeit a steep and tall one.

Slowly, with frequent pauses, the half-starved and nearly exhausted woman reached the summit of Anvil Rock. It took her most of a day, during which she had often been tempted to let herself fall, to exchange her suffering on the heights for surcease on jagged rocks or in icy depths below. With vehemence, Mary always afterward referred to this as her "most terrible day."

Fearful that her already overtaxed powers would fail her, Mary forced herself to begin her descent while it was yet light. From the summit of Anvil Rock there was a long, gradual slope to the east. Not far from its bottom she found a patch of corn. She shouted to bring its owners to her aid; there was no answer. But she had been heard. Soon three white men stood over her, Adam Harmon and his two sons, Mary's former neighbors at Draper's Meadows; after the massacre, they had moved about twelve miles west. The next thing Mary knew, she was in the Harmons' little cabin, swaddled in blankets and lying on a pallet before a cheery fire. Her lacerations had been bandaged. It was the first real shelter, the first warm clothing, the first bed, the first fire, the first decent food she had known in forty days.

During the next few days, Mary's periods of consciousness gradually lengthened between periods of deep sleep. Despite the fact that the Harmons' larder was full of venison haunches, Adam decided that what she needed was good English beef tea; he slaughtered one of his priceless cows to provide it.

When Mary was well enough to travel, Adam rode along with her the dozen miles to Draper's Meadows. The community had recovered remarkably since July 30, but its inhabitants had panicked at rumors of a new Indian raid and fled to the safety of a newly constructed fort at Dunkard's Bottom, near the spot where Will Ingles had recently established a ferry service across the New River.

At the fort, Mary's friends and neighbors greeted her first with disbelief and then with real joy. Her husband and her brother, John, were not there to welcome her, however. They had gone to seek information about their kidnapped wives from the Cherokees in northeastern Tennessee. Unknown to those at the fort, Will and John had completed their fruitless mission and had returned to within a few miles of Dunkard's Bottom. Their arrival at the small blockhouse the next morning was a wonderful reunion after nearly five months of separation.

Before Mary had recovered her strength in the Harmons' cabin, she had begged them to form a party to rescue Mrs. Bingamin from her mad wanderings on the west bank of the New River. The Harmons had been so horrified to learn that one of their neighbors had attacked another with cannibalistic intent that they had refused Mary's plea. But now they finally consented to look for Mrs. Bingamin. When they found her, she was nearby and in much better health than Mary had been, for she had found food, clothes, and a horse at a deserted cabin. When the two women met at Dunkard's Bottom they were quick to forgive each other. Because of renewed Indian raids, many homesteaders in the westernmost settlements retreated eastward. Most, like the Ingleses, moved only as far as Bedford, Virginia, about seventy-five miles east of Draper's Meadows. But the Bingamins pushed up the Shenandoah Valley to Winchester en route to Pennsylvania, and they never went back to Virginia. It is not unreasonable to suppose that they were ashamed of Mrs. Bingamin's threats against Mary, and that they decided to move away from the reproachful and suspicious eyes of their neighbors on the New River.

As the years went by and settlers penetrated farther into the western wilderness, word drifted back of the fate of the other captives. Eventually Mary learned, with a grief that no number of intervening years could soften, that her baby George had died within a year of his capture. But the others fared better. Betty Draper was found and ransomed some six years after Mary's return. Young Tom, too, came home, a long thirteen years after his good-bye to his mother. Will made many journeys into the Shawnee country before he tracked him down, and had to haggle long and hard before the lad's fellow braves would give him up.

Meanwhile, Will and Mary raised a large family. In the fullness of her years, Mary became the beloved matriarch of a considerable clan of grandchildren and great-grandchildren. She lived to be eighty-three. By the time she died, in 1815, she had seen the new United States born, and had watched it push its frontier westward. But she had been there first.

A "New and Strange Order of Men"

CONTINUED FROM PAGE 49

instance be compromised in subordinate altercations." Jefferson's enmity was dismissed by some defenders of the society as a bad case of sour grapes: he had not fought in the Revolution and was therefore ineligible for membership. Similar diagnoses were made for other critics of the order. But when Washington received a letter from Lafayette that gently but firmly criticized the hereditary clause of the Institution, he was impressed; normally a French nobleman could be expected to accept such things.

Clearly something had to be done to ease popular suspicions and end the divisive conflict. With a general meeting of the society scheduled for May of 1784 in Philadelphia, Washington decided to act. He went over the Institution line by line and wrote out a set of revisions meant, he noted, to "strike out every word, sentence and clause which has a political tendency." At the same time, he tried to enlist support for the coming convention. In one letter after another he urged Nathanael Greene to attend the meeting and use his prestige on the side of change. But Greene had political ambitions, and perhaps these pushed him toward discretion. He wrote to Washington: "The Doctor thinks my life would be endangered by attempting to cross the Water, and my pain in my stomach increased by riding by land." This bad news was balanced by word from Henry Knox, who agreed that the Institution would have to be revised. Determined to end the nation's cause for alarm, Washington left Mount Vernon at the end of April on his first long trip since the war's end.

Philadelphia welcomed him as a national hero, and his former officers showed themselves ready to accept his leadership. Speaking "warmly and in plain language," Washington persuaded the delegates to adopt a set of important changes in the Institution. After much debate, the convention voted to abolish both hereditary descent and honorary membership. It also decided to stop the political correspondence among state societies. The delegates agreed to wear society badges only at meetings, funerals of members, or in Europe, where they seemed more appropriate.

These concessions might have put an end to Washington's worries except for one circumstance. The Institution, modelled on the Articles of Confederation, had no provision for amendments. Before the changes could take effect, all thirteen of the state societies and the one in France as well had to ratify them. Three did so. Three refused. The remaining eight, including the one in France, first voted for revisions and then decided to support the original Institution. The

changes were disallowed. According to William S. Thomas, a historian of the Cincinnati, L'Enfant probably helped inspire the members' intransigence. His designs for a medal and a certificate had been made up in Paris, and he appeared in Philadelphia with some of the finished goods. "The Society was saved," comments Thomas. "Heartened delegates returned to their State Societies in a different frame of mind. . . ."

Fortunately for the order, the state societies were slow in voting; the rejection was not soon apparent. Washington did not learn that his reforms had been rejected until late in 1785. In December he expressed his irritation about the matter to Alexander Hamilton. His enthusiasm for the Cincinnati was at its lowest point, and he resolved to remain its nominal leader but to withdraw from its workings as much as possible.

Then fate intervened. A second general meeting of the society was set for Philadelphia in 1787—just, it developed, when the Constitutional Convention would be meeting to seek a more workable form of government. Washington had already notified the society that he would not be able to attend, giving rheumatism and pressing private affairs as his excuse. But now Jefferson, Madison, and Edmund Randolph were strongly urging his presence at the Constitutional Convention.

To a man of Washington's convictions, the overlapping conventions brought an agonizing dilemma. He clearly saw the need for a stronger government. Henry Knox warned him that there were "combustibles in every State, which a spark might set fire to." He himself feared that the spring of 1787 might bring scenes that would "astonish the world."

At the same time, the General's strict code of personal courtesy came into play. Washington was simply not a man who could now show up at the Cincinnati meeting and dismiss his earlier refusal with a wave of the hand. How, then, could he attend the Constitutional Convention without offending the society's leaders, who were, after all, his old comrades-in-arms? Finally he left for Philadelphia, having decided to attend both meetings.

As it turned out, his soul-searching was unnecessary. Once again the Cincinnati greeted him with great affection and respect, and things went well. He was re-elected president general with the understanding that Vice President Thomas Mifflin would handle all the active chores. And this time there was no testy public to contend with. Newspapers had widely publicized the revisions in the Institution proposed by the 1784 convention; but, unable to keep track of each state society's protracted voting, they happily had failed to report that the changes had not been adopted. For all the public knew, whatever dangers the Cincinnati presented had been eliminated three years before.

And in truth, even critics who knew that no changes had been made would have been hard put to build a serious case against the society. Its members were playing a prominent and positive role in the Constitutional Convention. Of the fifty-five original delegates, sixteen belonged to the order, and ten more became honorary members. Although Washington was distressed, as he wrote to a friend in 1788, to hear charges that "the proposed government [is] the wicked and traitorous fabrication of the Cincinnati," there was nothing to equal the outcry of 1783–84.

As time passed, the situation grew even calmer. When in 1790 General St. Clair named a town on the Ohio River in honor of the Cincinnati, no one objected strongly. Two years later Hugh Henry Brackenridge published a novel called *Modern Chivalry* in which he poked a satiric thumb in the society's eye, but he concluded that "it is a thing which can do little harm." The order itself at its 1790 meeting was glad to note: "It gives us inexpressible pleasure to find that the unreasonable and illogical clamor, which at one moment had been excited against our Institution, has totally subsided."

Even some of the more illustrious critics mellowed. Benjamin Franklin may have become an honorary member, although this point is not clear.* After the Cincinnati of South Carolina wrote to John Adams pledging its support during his Presidency, he commented: "When the Cincinnati of South Carolina pledge their lives, their fortunes, their sacred honor, I believe that no man will doubt their integrity."

Washington relaxed his wariness, and in time even the most severe critic of the Cincinnati found himself writing to the Virginia society to request funds for Central College, later to become the University of Virginia. But Thomas Jefferson's attacks had cut too deeply for quick healing; his request was rejected.

As for the order itself, any conspiratorial sparks smouldering in the membership were being doused in conviviality. In some state societies serious thoughts of preserving "union and national honor" gave ground to thoughts of meetings and picnics, usually held on the Fourth of July. On these occasions, noble sentiments were limited to a speech or two, and most of the energy went into shared reminiscences. In 1789,

officers of the Massachusetts society met at the Bunch of Grapes tavern in Boston to plan for the statewide meeting; the refreshment list would include "the best Madeira wine at fourteen shillings . . . per gallon, and the best claret wine at two shillings per bottle."

Not all state societies were so inclined to festiveness. At a typical Connecticut gathering in Hartford, members of the society marched soberly to a meetinghouse, where they first heard a prayer, then a reading of the Declaration of Independence. This was followed by an oration from one of the members, "sundry select pieces of sacred music . . . performed by the ladies and gentlemen of the City," and "a very elegant dinner composed of all the varieties of the season."

Neither type of meeting—wet or dry—seemed to

CINCINNATUS' FAMOUS SONS

The Cincinnati can boast a long list of prominent men among its hereditary and honorary members, and the range of their pursuits is as impressive as the men themselves. Washington and Monroe were original members; other Presidents to join were Jackson, Taylor, Pierce, Buchanan, Grant, Cleveland, Benjamin Harrison, McKinley, both Roosevelts, Taft, Wilson, Harding, Hoover, and Truman. A sampling of current hereditary members includes former Cabinet members C. Douglas Dillon and Sinclair Weeks; United States Senators Claiborne Pell, Hugh Scott, Thruston Morton, Richard Russell, and Samuel Ervin; drama critic and lecturer John Mason Brown; and Edgar F. Shannon, Jr., president of the University of Virginia. Among the present honorary members are Gustavus VI, King of Sweden; James F. Byrnes, former Secretary of State and former Supreme Court justice; J. Edgar Hoover; Generals Omar Bradley, Mark Clark, and Matthew Ridgway; historian Samuel Eliot Morison; and the Right Reverend Henry Knox Sherrill, former bishop of Massachusetts and retired presiding bishop of the Protestant Episcopal Church of the United States.

Not so long ago in Washington, D.C., there occurred the installation of a man whose maternal great-great-grandfather, Lieutenant Reuben Murray, had seen Revolutionary War service in regiments from New York and Connecticut, and had been a member of the Connecticut society.

As a number of distinguished guests looked on that day in 1952, Sir Winston Churchill received his badge and certificate with the comment that it was "a most memorable event in my crowded life." He then left a typical stamp on the proceedings by adding, "I am in the interesting situation of having fought on both sides in the war between us and we."

---

* The records of the Pennsylvania society say that Franklin was elected an honorary member on July 7, 1789, and there is an authentic certificate, dated July 11, 1789, bearing his name. However, another person's name had been erased from the diploma and Franklin's written in; thus the doubt about his membership.

The Society of the Cincinnati was created at Verplanck House, above, in the spring of 1783.

pose a clear threat to the Union. Nor did the society's everyday activities. As Revolutionary survivors grew old or ill, Cincinnati funds were provided for the support of widows, children, and other dependents. In time, the main business of meetings was passing on such cases. Certainly this was harmless. When the general convention of 1800 declared that the original Institution of 1783 was still in force, public reaction was nil. The society had become an accepted part of American life. Had it deserved all the condemnation? Had it really played a sinister role in the Republic's first fragile days?

Apparently not. During the critical 1780's it was, to be sure, a force for conservatism. Since many members held public bonds, they supported Alexander Hamilton's idea that a government must not renege on its obligations. The society opposed Shays' Rebellion; indeed, the uprising was finally crushed by soldiers under Benjamin Lincoln, president of the Massachusetts society, and Henry Knox proudly reported to Washington that "the few wretched officers who were against the government were not of the Cincinnati."

Given their financial outlook and inherent conservatism, it is not surprising that many society members found themselves allied with the Federalists. In fact, the society could hardly have been better represented in the constitutional government during its early years. George Washington, of course, was both President of the United States and president general of the society. Henry Knox was his Secretary of War, Alexander Hamilton his Secretary of the Treasury. Timothy Pickering served terms as Postmaster General, Secretary of War, and Secretary of State.

Hamilton, with his sound-money views, seems to have attracted an especially warm following in the society. During the 1790's, Antifederalists even accused the Cincinnati of being a "machine" to push Hamilton's political ambitions. These fears were not eased when in 1800 Hamilton became president general to fill the place created by Washington's death. Four years

later, however, all such worries were ended by the pistol of another Cincinnati member, Aaron Burr.

But the order in itself was never a potent political force. In the early years of the nineteenth century it supported a plan that would have given half-pay for life to officers of Washington's army. The Cincinnati's secretary general, William Jackson, acted as official lobbyist for the drive and developed some of the pressure techniques that perhaps inspired later veterans' groups. In 1826 Congress finally granted full pay for life to all officers still around to collect it. However, the society could not claim full credit for this action.

Indeed, at this time the order was in tatters. Public hostility had scared off some members. Death or indifference had taken many others. Only six of the state societies were active, and the branch in France had long since been sawed off by the French Revolution.* Moreover, the Cincinnati had helped its own decline by refusing to admit any state society outside the first thirteen. With former officers and their descendants moving westward, and with means of communication at a rudimentary level, many people simply could not maintain their ties.

Dust settled and cobwebs formed. In November, 1854, the last original member of the society died. His name was Robert Burnett and, fittingly or ironically, he breathed his last in Newburgh, New York, where Washington had faced his restive officers and where he had agreed to lead the Cincinnati. By this time, things were so low that the order voted to take in descendants of Continental officers who had been eligible for membership in 1783 but had not joined up.

Like a retired campaigner in the doze of his late years, the order slumbered. Then it was reawakened—by the rising tide of immigration. As wave upon wave of hopeful foreigners rolled into the country, people began climbing their family trees to escape the plebeian flood. The past became fashionable, especially if one's own family was involved. Up sprang such

* At first, radical Frenchmen considered the Cincinnati a symbol of liberty. On July 12, 1789, two days before the storming of the Bastille, a rebel named Camille Desmoulins mounted a table in Paris and proposed that a cockade be chosen to represent the popular movement. Casting about among suitable colors, he cried, "What shall it be? Shall it be green, the color of hope, or shall it be blue, the color of the Cincinnati?" Voices in the excited crowd shouted back, "Let it be green, the color of hope."

When green was later discovered to be the color of Louis XVI's brother, red and blue, the colors of Paris, were substituted. Then Lafayette suggested that a strip of the old national white be added—and thus helped create the famous tricolor.

Lafayette's prestige was so high at this point that he was able to send a key of the fallen Bastille to George Washington. However, France's Cincinnati, formed almost exclusively of nobility, did not survive the Terror. Many members died on the guillotine, including the society's president, Comte d'Estaing. After one slaughter, the horse of a terrorist was decorated with Cincinnati badges taken from executed owners.

organizations as the Sons of the American Revolution and its awesome counterpart, the Daughters.

With its aristocratic beginnings and hereditary rules, membership in the Cincinnati carried with it a set of impeccable social credentials. Grandsons and great-grandsons found themselves nudging the society's comatose body. During the 1880's and 1890's it was revived and fitted out in a handsome new uniform. The old boy was back in business.

The society became a kind of first of the first families of America. Great attention was paid to ceremony, and meeting after meeting concerned itself with such problems as the wearing of the badge (around the neck for entertainments, and over the left breast for business, decided the general meeting at Richmond in 1905). News of these concerns was bound to get about, and the society inspired men to poetry. Wrote Arthur Guiterman in a 1936 issue of *The New Yorker*:

> The D.A.R.lings
> Chatter like starlings
> Telling their ancestors' names,
> While grimly aloof
> With looks of reproof,
> Sit the Colonial Dames.
>
> And The Cincinnati
> All merry and chatty
> Dangle their badges and pendants,
> But haughty and proud
> Disdaining the crowd
> Brood the Mayflower Descendants.

Social impeccability, however, did not always guarantee current acceptability. Cleveland Amory reports in *Who Killed Society* that *Life* magazine sent a photographer-reporter team to cover the 1956 triennial meeting of the society at Newport, Rhode Island. Finding no one of marketable interest—that is, no one "who talked at cocktails while a group of proper-looking people gathered around and hung on every word" —the *Life* men departed.

With or without *Life*'s approval, the Cincinnati today is flourishing. All fourteen of its societies are active. The total membership has reached 2,400 and is still growing. Verplanck House burned down in 1931, but the society maintains Anderson House in Washington, D.C., as a combination headquarters and museum. The order's most recent triennial meeting was held at Princeton, New Jersey, last May.

Unlike some other patriotic societies, the order works quietly in its dealings with the outside world. The French society having been restored in 1925, the Cincinnati now finances a trip to America for a young Frenchman—preferably a member of the order or the descendant of a member—to study American civilization at Harvard Summer School and to take a non-academic tour of inspection around the country. In 1959 the Cincinnati held its triennial meeting in France and had a reception at Louis XIV's old pomping grounds, the palace of Versailles. Some members even met with General Charles de Gaulle, a modern sun king who did not choose to follow the example of Cincinnatus. Down through the years the society has taken an active interest in American history. It helped transfer the remains of Nathanael Greene, John Paul Jones, and George Clinton to suitable resting places. In 1804 it paid for John Trumbull's painting of George Washington. It led the fight to preserve the U.S.S. *Constellation*. It built and maintains a monument at New Windsor, New York, where preliminary plans for the order were thrashed out and made final.

Today the society has many activities. Its invaluable collection of Revolutionary documents and papers is kept in the Library of Congress, and Anderson House is an interesting museum in its own right. In keeping with one of its original aims, the society still gives financial help to needy members. In addition, the state societies have their own programs. Virginia's gives fellowships to several colleges and universities within the state. Connecticut's presents a sword to an outstanding graduate of the Coast Guard Academy at New London. Others mark historical sites and help maintain library rooms devoted to U.S. history.

Who could object to such activities? It is hard to imagine that Jefferson would find much to rail against now. Probably his fears were not justified in the first place, for as Franklin realized, the Cincinnati might well have gone unnoticed if it had not been for the hereditary clause and the badges of membership. A weakness for pomp and a certain naïveté about public reactions is not unknown among military men. But by assuming an aristocratic air, no matter how innocent, the founders tweaked a tender nerve in the young nation and got a violent twitch in return.

Nowadays the military influence in American life assumes guises that would have astonished the men at Verplanck House. If Cincinnatus had lived in this age, he doubtless would have retired from the battlefield and slipped into the board chairmanship of some leading firm in the defense industry. Grateful senators could then have rewarded him not with a wreath but with a contract.

Mr. Hoey, whom we are pleased to welcome to our pages, is senior editor of Read *magazine, a periodical used in junior high schools; he lives in Middletown, Connecticut. The many sources for his article included two books by William S. Thomas:* Members of the Society of the Cincinnati *(Tobias A. Wright, Inc., 1929) and* The Society of the Cincinnati *(Putnam, 1935).*

Lomasney saw to it that Ward Eight was clean. There was no vice, gambling, rough stuff, no trouble about votes. Both the quick and the dead voted to his order, but he did not take graft. Money to run the Hendricks Club services came from two sources. Those who got jobs understood, although it was never mentioned, that something was expected in return. Lomasney also accepted donations from all concerns that did business in the West End. The firms made their donations voluntarily, even cheerfully, but they might have found reason to regret it if they had not.

There was surprise when the Mahatma decreed that he was backing Fitzgerald. Fitzgerald was almost unanimously elected and spent two unspectacular years in the Senate quietly building up his machine for the next leap forward, using his statehouse opportunities to settle relatives and strategic supporters in plush jobs. With exemplary patriotism he sponsored the April 19 anniversary of the battles of Lexington and Concord as a local holiday; and with an eye to the Italians now appearing on the waterfront, he wangled the same favor for Columbus Day in October. In 1894, moving crabwise but with his eye permanently fixed on City Hall, Fitzgerald announced his candidacy for Congress. Again Lomasney backed him, opposing Congressman Joseph O'Neil, who was supported by most of the other ward bosses. It was a rough election as the Irish wards knew elections, but with the solid support of Wards Six and Eight, Johnny Fitz, "the boy candidate," was not to be beaten.

Fitzgerald served as a congressman for three terms. He made no name for himself; his chief concern in Congress was to expand his political power in Boston. Brother Henry in the North End kept the machine well-supplied with oil. During the Washington years, Johnny bought a house in rural Concord, but he still kept his legal address in the North End.

In the 1895 election the time was not yet for another Irish mayor. Boston's ward bosses picked and elected Josiah Quincy, a Yankee Democrat. Three bosses—no friends of Lomasney's—did the picking: "Smiling Jim" Donovan, the chairman of the Democratic City Committee; Judge Joseph J. Corbett, the election commissioner; and East Boston's Patrick "P. J." Kennedy. Impressed by the rise of Fitzgerald, they were willing—if he would turn his back on the Mahatma—to admit the Congressman to their circle as the fourth mayor-maker. Honey Fitz was willing.

In 1901 the Big Four, still biding their own time, managed to persuade the austerely respectable Patrick Collins to be the Democratic candidate. Collins was easily if reluctantly elected. He always found the job of mayor distasteful. Smiling Jim he made superintendent of streets, but refused most other patronage demands. Johnny Fitz galled him.

Meanwhile Fitzgerald had bought a moribund neighborhood paper, the *Republic,* for five hundred dollars. This he turned into an Irish-American social weekly which he both edited and published. Nothing in it was of any great interest, nor did readers flock to it. Nevertheless, department stores, public utilities, and contractors hurried to buy half and full page advertisements. In spite of its small circulation and stiff rates, the *Republic* was soon netting its new publisher $25,000 a year.

In 1903 Fitzgerald moved back from Concord to Dorchester, a Boston suburb. The house he bought on Welles Avenue was a wooden château with a scrollwork porch, blank plate-glass windows, and a mansard turret. On the stair landing he had a stained-glass window installed with a Fitzgerald coat of arms and the Gaelic motto *Shawn A Boo,* "John the Bold."

John the Bold, full of bounce and pugnacious confidence, knew that the municipal election year of 1905 was his year. Every ward heeler and precinct worker sensed instinctively that Johnny Fitz would be a candidate, would be indeed *the* candidate for mayor. Collins had died that September, and the question for the bosses was: whom should they run against this dynamic challenger they had built up a decade before? Smiling Jim and P. J. turned to the Mahatma, and they picked City Clerk Edward Donovan.

Impelled from the clerk's office to the hustings, Donovan scarcely knew what hit him. Johnny Fitz was off like a whirlwind on the most blatantly spectacular campaign Boston's twenty-four wards had ever seen. Vacant walls were pasted with his posters twice as fast as opponents could tear them down. "Bigger, Better, Busier Boston" was emblazoned under the smiling Fitzgerald phiz, retouched to benignity by the photographer. The city marvelled at the roar of the first political motorcade. Honey Fitz toured the wards in a large red car, followed by flying squads of what the reporters described as "Napoleon's lancers," and was met in each precinct by crowds of militant Dearos.

For weeks Johnny Fitz made ten speeches a night, denouncing the bosses and the "machine," and on the evening before the primaries he reached the almost breathless total of thirty. But for Lomasney he would have buried Donovan. Fitzgerald won the nomination, carrying twenty of the city's wards, but it took a dozen wards to make up the votes he lost in Ward Eight.

The reform Republicans and the Good Government Association—a civic organization founded two years before by the Chamber of Commerce, the Merchants Association, the Associated Board of Trade, the Fruit and Produce Association, the New England Shoe and Leather Association, and the Bar Association—had succeeded in nominating the highly respected speaker of the Massachusetts House of Representatives, Louis Frothingham. Unreformed Republicans, with the concealed moral and financial encouragement of Fitzgerald, ran Judge Henry Dewey—already beaten by Frothingham in the primaries—as an independent Republican.

Frothingham represented all the things that Fitzgerald could ring the sour changes on—Harvard, blue blood, inherited wealth. Honey Fitz also spread thickly the unjustified rumor that his opponent was anti-Catholic and anti-Irish. He kept up his whirlwind campaign with variations, visiting department stores and glad-handing the salespeople, even inaugurating a "soda water campaign" with ice-cream sodas and refreshments for women's groups in critical wards.

The battle cost Fitzgerald $120,000—twice as much as it did Frothingham. "But it was not money which won the campaign," George K. Turner wrote in *Collier's*. "It was action, ingenuity, and boundless, cheerful effrontery. For thirteen years Johnny Fitz had held Ward Six obedient and cheerful by public jobs. He extended that one basic system of ward politics over all the city."

The new mayor took possession of the gray mock-Renaissance City Hall on School Street like a conqueror exacting the submission of a defeated town. The Mayor himself kept control of all the city departments except the schools and the police. He replaced a physician with a saloonkeeper on the Board of Health; he appointed another saloonkeeper superintendent of public buildings; a whitewasher, superintendent of sewers; a bartender who had been expelled from the legislature, superintendent of streets. For deserving Dearos he created new offices such as that of city dermatologist. Eight additional deputy sealers were added to the Department of Weights and Measures—a department soon to erupt in open scandal. The vestiges of civil service were circumvented by the invention of novel job categories—tea warmers, tree climbers, wipers, rubber-boot repairers, watchmen to watch other watchmen.

In Johnny Fitz's first administration, graft was blatant in all departments. During those two years the city lost $200,000 in dealings with a single coal company, whose manager later absconded. In subsequent investigations the Finance Commission discovered that Boston had been paying sixty cents a barrel more than the going price for cement—a $240,000 annual waste. There were dozens of strange land deals in which the

city ended up paying three times more than anyone had imagined a given property was worth.

For most of the time the accumulating scandals seemed secondary to the dynamic ubiquitousness of the little man in the mayor's chair. During his first term he is estimated to have attended 1,200 dinners, 1,500 dances, 200 picnics, and 1,000 meetings; made 3,000 speeches; and danced with 5,000 girls. He thought up Old Home Week and applied it first to Boston—even though Beacon Street held aloof. With his entourage he liked to drop in for a sudden meal, amidst the flattering bustle of the staff, at the various city hotels—the Adams and Parker houses; Young's; Quincy House, the Democratic politicians' eyrie on the fringe of the North End; the Winter Palace; and the South End's naughtily Edwardian Woodcock. The Mayor excelled as a greeter, entertaining personally such varied visitors as Prince Wilhelm of Sweden and the magician Houdini. Between 1905 and 1907, Johnny Fitz made himself a city institution.

Two years of Fitzgerald, however, brought an inevitable reaction. There were still transplanted Irish in Boston who felt that Patrick Collins had been a worthier representative than Johnny Fitz and his Dearos. They remembered how Collins as mayor had welcomed the delegates of the National Municipal League and asked them to report to him if they found anything shady in his administration. What they might have found in Fitz's did not bear thinking about.

For the 1907 elections anti-Fitzgerald Democrats nominated Representative John Coulthurst. Coulthurst also had the backing of Hearst's *American* and of all the bosses except Lomasney, who this time returned to Johnny Fitz. The Republicans picked their own variety of boss, George A. Hibbard, the Boston postmaster. Hibbard was a parrot-nosed, thrifty Yankee who announced he was running for one term solely for the purpose of "cleaning up the mess." Fitzgerald conducted his usual bouncing, badgering campaign, adding such *bizarreries* as circulars in Yiddish to persuade the newly arrived Jewish voters. In a narrow election, Coulthurst swung enough Democrats from Fitzgerald so that Hibbard was able to win.

Mayor Hibbard, while looking after needy Republicans, did much of what he had promised. He cut down the municipal payroll, halved the cost of street maintenance, and reduced the city's debt. Through departmental efficiencies he managed to save about a million dollars. Toward the end of his administration, and in the hope of more reform mayors to come, the Good Government Association maneuvered the adoption of a new city charter. According to its terms, party designations were to be dropped from the municipal ballot. There were to be no more primaries, and nominations for mayor could be made by voters' petition. A nine-member council would replace the thirteen aldermen and seventy-five councillors. The mayor's term was lengthened to four years.

Electorates soon weary of reform interludes, however, and those who are barred from the trough weary even sooner. By 1909 it seemed that the wheel had turned and that the colorless Hibbard would be replaced by Johnny Fitz. To avoid four more years of Fitzgerald entrenchment, Republicans and reformers united on the bluest blood of Beacon Street, James Jackson Storrow. A predestined Harvard man, Storrow had been captain of a crew that had beaten Yale, and he was now New England's wealthiest banker. Although imposing in figure, he was a poor speaker. This was offset by his being that atavistic anomaly, a Yankee Democrat.

Smiling Jim Donovan early threw in his lot with Storrow, impressing on the banker the truism that political campaigns cost money. Storrow was impressed— he gave a half million dollars before his campaign was over. Storrow money was loosely plentiful, and Smiling Jim understood its application. Curley, then the visibly rising boss of the South End's Ward Seventeen, said later that he had refused $60,000 to side with Storrow. Fitzgerald knew that without the support of Curley and Lomasney he could not win. The three came to an agreement. The thirty-five-year-old Curley as junior partner was to take over Fitzgerald's old congressional seat and bide his time in Washington until the next municipal election. What Lomasney was offered remains a secret.

"Take Storrow's money, but vote for Fitzgerald,"

was the word the Dearos passed round. Storrow tried to argue about corruption and the issues of municipal government. Johnny Fitz simplified the election into a contest between an Irish-Catholic boy from the slums and a wealth-encrusted Harvard blue blood who was anti-Catholic, anti-labor, anti-Negro, and anti- anything else Fitzgerald could think of between speeches. He papered the city with large photographs of City Hall on which was inscribed: NOT FOR SALE, MR. $TORROW. "Manhood against Money" was another Fitzgerald slogan that was used under a touchingly domestic photograph of Fitz and his family.

In a day when a political meeting was for many the most entertaining event of the year, Johnny Fitz was a circus and a prophet combined. During the frenzied weeks before the election he led his motorcade through several thousand miles of shabby streets, shouting his tenor voice hoarse in halls and on corners. Fitzgerald even persuaded Hibbard, mortally ill, to run as a token candidate to draw votes from Storrow.

The Saturday night before the election Fitzgerald staged his biggest and most bumptious rally in Faneuil Hall in the North End. As an added attraction he had hired a brass band, instructing the leader to play "The Star-Spangled Banner" at his entrance and to follow it up with "The Wearing of the Green." The latter song concluded, however, before Fitzgerald and his entourage could manage to handshake their way to the platform. In the interlude, because it was a popular song of the moment, and with nothing more in mind, the leader had the bank strike up "Sweet Adeline." Everybody joined in the chorus. When it came time for the second verse, Johnny Fitz with deft spontaneity capered down the platform and sang it solo, then led the crowd again in the chorus. And in that bellowing moment of beaming fair faces the "Honey Fitz" legend was born. Ever after that, whenever the speeches began to run dry at a Democratic meeting, the cry would go up for Honey Fitz to sing "Sweet Adeline."

It was generally admitted by politicians afterward

A 1913 cartoon portrayed Honey Fitz as Napoleon, and James M. Curley, with his mayoralty aspirations, as Victoriano Huerta, an insurgent Mexican politico of the period. From an early stance of bold defiance, Fitzgerald soon moved to withdraw from the race; Curley won the election.

that Honey Fitz's demonic gusto in the last few days of the campaign won him the election. On the final night he spoke at thirty-five rallies, and topped it off by singing "Sweet Adeline" from the roof of a hack. Even so, in the largest vote in Boston's history, he barely squeaked through with 47,177 votes to 45,775 for Storrow. The ailing Hibbard, repudiated by the Republicans, received only 1,614 votes—enough, however, to have elected Storrow.

Not much could be said about Honey Fitz's second term as mayor that was not said about his first, except that Boston was used to it. And there were solid accomplishments, whatever their price tag. Honey Fitz built the City Hall Annex, the City Point Aquarium, numberless public convenience stations memorialized with his name, and the Franklin Park Zoo. He founded the High School of Commerce to prepare for the business world boys who could not go to college. He also inaugurated the banned-in-Boston tradition by forbidding the turkey trot and the tango as immoral, *Salome* as sacrilegious, and the red flag in parades as both.

Greeting and entertaining were his official delights. At City Hall he welcomed such assorted figures as the French actress Gaby Deslys, New Jersey's Governor Woodrow Wilson, William Jennings Bryan, Theodore Roosevelt, Lady Gregory, and the lord mayors of Dublin and London. Sir Thomas Lipton relaxed in his company, visiting him not only in Dorchester but also in the Fitzgerald gingerbread ark of a summer house in Hull, overlooking Boston Harbor. In 1914 Honey Fitz's oldest daughter, Rose, married a brashly up-and-coming young Harvard graduate, Joseph Patrick Kennedy, the son of East Boston's P. J.

Honey Fitz had made a bosses' agreement to leave City Hall at the end of his term. He toyed briefly with the quixotic notion of running for governor or even for United States senator, but as his pleasant and profitable months in the gray School Street building ran out he began to feel that his earlier renunciation was premature. Meanwhile, Congressman Curley, rounding out his second term in Washington, was regarding the gilt eagle on top of City Hall with an increasingly cold and calculating eye. "You are an old man," he told the forty-nine-year-old mayor by way of a Curley-type hint. "Get your slippers and pipe and stretch out in your hammock and read the *Ladies' Home Journal.*"

The lone wolf of Ward Seventeen was the one opponent whom Honey Fitz feared. Unlike most politicians, Curley never developed a nickname. Even though he had begun by imitating the Ward Six Napoleon, he had been brought up in a harder school. He had a more commanding presence and a more resonant voice, a crueller tongue and a quicker fist.

Honey Fitz may have been meaner, but Curley was tougher, and he had the instinct for the jugular.

In November, 1913, Curley let it be known officially that he would be a candidate for mayor in January's election. A few weeks before Christmas Honey Fitz made the announcement that he had decided to run for another term. Next day the Boston *Post* quoted Curley's comment: "Fitzgerald wants a licking, and he will get it." The two were now archenemies, and though from time to time there were superficial political gestures of good will, they were to remain enemies.

Not long after Honey Fitz's announcement, Curley announced that he would give three lectures contrasting famous characters of history with John F. Fitzgerald. His first lecture, given at the Dorchester high school, was on "Graft in Ancient Times vs. Graft in Modern Times," with comparisons between the Rome of the Caesars and the Boston of the Dearos. The next lecture was advertised as "Great Lovers: From Cleopatra to Toodles," but before it could be given, Honey Fitz had withdrawn his candidacy.

Toodles Ryan was a cigarette girl at the Ferncroft Inn, one of Honey Fitz's ports of call along the Newburyport Turnpike. He had met her there some years before. Afterward there was a blur of talk about the Mayor and the shapely blonde. In later years Honey Fitz righteously insisted in a statement to the *Post* that he had never done more than kiss Toodles casually and publicly during a large party at which his wife was present. Curley to the contrary, those close to Honey Fitz have always maintained that the Toodles stories were no more than malicious jokes.

After Honey Fitz's withdrawal, he and the ward bosses—with the exception of Lomasney—united incongruously with the Good Government Association on an anti-Curley candidate, City Councillor Thomas J. Kenny, an honest but uninspired budget expert who had once served on the school committee. At the last moment P. J. Kennedy shifted his support to Curley. In spite of the opposition of the rest of the bosses—whom Curley now swore to destroy—the young man from the South End was unbeatable.

With Curley's election, Honey Fitz's office-holding days came to an end. Though he would live on for a third of a century, though he would several times be a candidate, he would not again achieve public place. But he remained a potent political figure in Boston.

For some time he enjoyed his leisure. He could indulge in his passion for long auto rides, for cruising in Boston Harbor, and for sporting events—baseball, football, prize fights. With the approach of winter he sunned himself in Florida. His social life buzzed much as ever. He dined and he danced, he spoke and he sang. In 1915 he received an honorary doctorate of laws from Notre Dame University, and liked afterward to be referred to as Dr. Fitzgerald. But by 1916 he could feel the old political stirrings in his blood.

That year was the first in Massachusetts for direct election of United States senators, and Henry Cabot Lodge, who had served three terms by vote of the Massachusetts legislature, was forced to take his chances with the electorate. In the wake of Wilson's presidential victory a Yankee Democrat could probably have defeated Lodge that year. Not, however, Honey Fitz. Fitzgerald managed to win the Democratic nomination, but Lodge won the election.

After that the road led downhill. Honey Fitz ran for various offices without success, sporadically announced and then withdrew his candidacy, and imperceptibly but surely began that mellowing process by which politicians and other wayward characters become fixtures, so that even their old enemies are glad to see them. P. J. Kennedy died in 1929. Lomasney followed shortly after Roosevelt's first inauguration. Only the indestructible Curley remained, alternately winning and losing elections. In 1937, with wry pride, Honey Fitz saw his son-in-law appointed ambassador to Great Britain.

Although no one admitted it openly, it was obvious by the forties that the last of the Dearos was slipping. At his eighty-first birthday party at the Parker House a congratulatory message arrived from the White House, addressed to Boston's Number One Booster. The climax of the party came when Honey Fitz's grandson, Navy Lieutenant John F. Kennedy, suddenly walked into the room, lean and yellow but buoyantly alive after surviving the loss of his PT boat and an attack of malaria.

After his discharge from the Navy, Jack Kennedy came to Boston and let it be known that he would run for Congress from his grandfather's old district. Grandfather and grandson spent hours together, Honey Fitz retelling his old political sagas, giving advice; but Jack with his Harvard background and his clipped speech represented a new breed of Irish-American. The supporters and strategists who gathered around him were Democrats in the liberal New Deal image, lean young men, college-educated, most of them ex-officers, many from private schools, with only their surnames to show kinship with the old. Kennedy won the election easily. Honey Fitz danced a jig on top of a table, sang a quavering "Sweet Adeline," and proudly predicted that his grandson would eventually be President.

Honey Fitz lived long enough to celebrate his diamond wedding and to see Jack overwhelmingly reelected to Congress, but not quite long enough to see him triumph in 1952 over Senator Henry Cabot Lodge, Jr., the grandson of his old Brahmin adversary. James Michael Curley outlived Honey Fitz by almost a decade. In a few years it seemed they both had been gone a generation. Boston, laid waste and rebuilt through urban renewal, was no longer the city they had known when the highest building was the Custom House. The baths and convenience stations they had built to perpetuate their names had vanished like the derbies they once wore. Only Honey Fitz's wife, Josephine Mary, lived on to see his capering prophecy fulfilled as his grandson and namesake became President of the United States. When Jack was in Boston he often used to visit her. She died at the age of ninety-eight, twenty-one months after her grandson's assassination, without ever having been told about it.

When I was five years old I met Honey Fitz, a little over a year after Curley had driven him from public life. My father had taken me to some political reception in Dorchester Lower Mills with the promise that if I behaved myself I should meet the "ex-Mayor." "Ex-Mayor" had a magic sound, and I envisioned him as a stately being in a sweeping velvet gown with a gold chain of office round his neck. "Where is the ex-Mayor?" I kept badgering my father, until I finally saw before my disbelieving eyes the brusque, dumpy figure in the brown striped suit that was John F. Fitzgerald. Honey Fitz may have been a ladies' man, but he obviously had no great liking for children. He exchanged a few words with my father, gave me a perfunctory pat on the head, and turned away. I was too disappointed to speak.

I never met his grandson Jack. The one time I saw him was when as a congressman he was running against Senator Lodge in 1952. With members of the Democratic State Committee and Governor Dever he stood on the platform at Springfield, welcoming Adlai Stevenson to Massachusetts. Those assembled politicians were of the second generation, heavy-jowled, heavy-paunched, the shoulders of their suits vast and padded, their ties hand-painted in rainbow tints. Stevenson, the mutely dressed academic Hamlet, and the third-generation congressman in his narrow-shouldered suit and regimental-stripe tie, seemed from another world. Kennedy looked like what indeed he would shortly become, the youngest member of the Harvard Board of Overseers. Watching him I suddenly realized that in this young man moving rather elegantly among the "pols" the consolidation of a new class had reached its conclusion.

Francis Russell, a veteran contributor to AMERICAN HERITAGE, *is the author of a biography of Warren G. Harding to be published this fall by McGraw-Hill.*

READING, WRITING, AND HISTORY

By BRUCE CATTON

Struggling Against Empire

A little less than three quarters of a century ago America had a presidential election marked by a passionate argument over American involvement in Asia. As a result of the "splendid little war" with Spain, the country found that it possessed an empire in the Far East; found also that it was deeply involved in the international politics of the Orient, was fighting to suppress a guerrilla war waged by men of a different color,* and altogether was following a course that seemed to have very little in common with American traditions, American ideals, or the precepts of the Founding Fathers.

It was perplexing and disturbing, and a number of prominent Americans correctly believed that it would have long-range consequences that some subsequent generation would find extremely difficult. As members of the subsequent generation most painfully involved in these consequences, we today can perhaps learn something by examining the anti-imperialist campaign that accompanied the election of 1900.

A stimulating text is at hand—Robert L. Beisner's thought-provoking book *Twelve Against Empire: The Anti-Imperialists, 1898–1900*, which reviews that unavailing effort to check an irresistible tide and succeeds admirably both in showing what the anti-imperialists were fighting against and why at last they failed.

The hard core of the anti-imperialist movement

* One aspect of that war is described in "Pershing's Island War," beginning on page 32 of this issue.

was provided by the Mugwumps—those public men, mostly wellborn and well-heeled, like William James, E. L. Godkin, Charles Eliot Norton, Charles Francis Adams, Jr., and Carl Schurz, who ever since the abolition of slavery had been reformers in search of a cause. They were joined by such Republican dissidents as Senator George F. Hoar, Andrew Carnegie, Benjamin Harrison, and Thomas B. Reed, united, more or less, in the 1900 campaign by a conviction that "the very purpose and destiny of the nation" were now at stake.

They saw America entering the perilous stream of power politics. In their eyes this ended a century of "free security" for America and marked "the beginning of a new epoch of war and international crisis." They were convinced that if the Republic followed this course it could not be true to its heritage, and they were fond of repeating the Mugwump saying that "Dewey took Manila with the loss of one man— and all our institutions."

Politically, their campaign never had a chance. The cards were all stacked the wrong way. The Republican candidate was President William McKinley, under whose guidance (or at least with whose acquiescence) the whole expansionist program had come to flower; and McKinley's running mate was Theodore Roosevelt, who seemed to be the very high priest of rising imperialism. The Democratic candidate was William Jennings Bryan, who blew both hot and cold: he opposed annexation of the Philippines, then from some foggy notion of smart political tactics supported the treaty which confirmed annexation, returned to his original position, and in the campaign devoted himself chiefly to the domestic issues about which he had been so eloquent four years earlier. Besides, McKinley was defending the full dinner pail, Bryan still believed in free silver, imperialism was only one of many issues, and it does not take a political expert to see why the electorate went Republican.

Beyond that, as Mr. Beisner makes clear, the Mugwumps themselves abysmally lacked the talent for mass leadership. They had an irritating way of standing above the battle. They believed that they spoke for the best thought and the best culture in the land, they made no attempt to conceal this belief, they actually had little political influence, and in the end they sadly concluded that "America had lost much of its fineness" because it rejected their counsel. At times they looked altogether too much like men who wanted to lead a revolt of the upper classes against the rising power of America. They lacked the common touch chiefly because they had no understanding of the common people.

Furthermore, as reformers born and bred, they wholly neglected the crucial domestic problems of the day—the central social and political issues that racked post-Civil War America. As William Allen White once unkindly remarked, they wanted reform "only in a certain vague, inarticulate, bullfrog fashion." And, finally, they were just a little confused about the basis for their opposition to the American presence in the Philippines. It was never entirely clear whether they thought we ought to be out of the islands because it was morally wrong for us to be in them or just because the islands were so infernally far away. They consented readily enough to American expansionism in the Caribbean. As Mr. Beisner remarks, without the

---

Twelve Against Empire: The Anti-Imperialists, 1898–1900, by Robert L. Beisner. McGraw-Hill Book Company. 294 pp. $6.95.

Philippines the whole anti-imperialist move probably would never have got off the ground. It failed, in short, to answer the question that is still bothering us today: do we propose to get out of Asia on high moral grounds or because staying there is just too big a job for us to handle?

Nevertheless, the anti-imperialists were right on the basic issue: going fully armored into the international arena, America was fated to become something different than it had been before, with grave risk to its ancient traditions. The splendid little war that was won so easily left us in permanent possession of Pandora's box, and when we went into the Philippines we took the lid off it. We are still looking for a way to get the lid back on.

The Balance of Power

The catch in all of this is that the lid was coming off Pandora's box anyway. At the close of the nineteenth century the United States and the world at large were changing in such a way that America was going to be involved in power politics no matter what it did in the Caribbean or in Asia. From Dewey's victory in Manila Bay to the announcement of the Truman Doctrine in 1947—which can be taken as the more or less formal beginning of the Cold War—was just a half century, and that half century had seen a profound shift in the whole international power structure. When President Truman pledged this country to "support free peoples who are resisting attempted subjugation by armed minorities or by outside pressures," he was taking a step that was logically connected with what the McKinley administration did in 1898, but it was a step that almost certainly would have been forced upon us even if the McKinley administration had behaved differently.

Thus an excellent book to read in connection with Mr. Beisner's work is Louis J. Halle's *The Cold War as History*. Mr. Halle here undertakes to examine the Cold War from a detached viewpoint, discussing it precisely as a historian might do a century afterward. The book is written as if the Cold War were something we had already lived through, an affair that had not only a beginning but an end. The end, to be sure, has unfortunately not yet arrived, and yet Mr. Halle believes that it is in sight; or, at least, that the time of greatest danger has already passed. It is nice to find someone so hopeful; meanwhile, *The Cold War as History* does shed a good deal of light on the eventful half-century between McKinley and Truman, and it is worth reading even by those who may not share Mr. Halle's optimism.

What Mr. Halle begins with is the assertion that by the end of the nineteenth century "the foundations of the long-standing world order on which American detachment depended were crumbling." America had been able to be detached because of the long stability of the balance of power in Europe. In terms of power, Europe until then was the whole world, and its balance of power was a world balance. America could remain happily isolated as long as that balance existed.

In other words, says Mr. Halle, our detachment from international power politics rested on the great Pax Britannica, because the European balance of power had been maintained largely by British naval supremacy. But as the 1890's ended, that supremacy was beginning to come to an end; Germany, Japan, and the United States itself were becoming strong naval powers, as a result of which Europe's balance was no longer in equilibrium. The British navy was no longer omnipotent, and so the New World was no longer strategically detached. Now America found itself involved in power politics in a way and to an extent no American had foreseen—not because it had thoughtlessly taken on an empire in Asia, but because the whole world had changed.

The great lesson of World War I, as Mr. Halle remarks, was that the chief responsibility for policing the balance of power now lay with us. We ignored the lesson, tried to return to our traditional isolation, and eventually found ourselves in World War II—which, essentially, was a fight to re-establish a stable power structure. After both of these wars, America tried to devise an alternative to power politics, Woodrow Wilson bringing forth the League of Nations, Franklin Roosevelt the United Nations. Neither succeeded, and both of them, in Mr. Halle's view, simply reflected "the naïveté of the American mind in the first half of the century."

And the Cold War (to continue with Mr. Halle's argument) developed because World War II left a power vacuum—military, economic, and political—in Europe. We had fought to eliminate German power and had succeeded; England was exhausted, France was itself part of the vacuum, the vacuum had to be filled by something, and across Europe came the Russian armies. This in turn pulled the United States back to Europe, back into international affairs everywhere, and there developed what Mr. Halle considers the central condition of the Cold War—the mutual opposition of two Europes, one led by Russia, the other by America.

At which point we start looking again toward Asia. For this reason: "Europe had offered solid ground on which the United States could make a stand. By contrast, Asia was a swamp." There was a common understanding with the Europeans; with the Asiatics there was none whatever. And this, the author suggests, blinded us to the fact that the Cold War was essentially "a spasm . . . brought on by a collapse of the Western power structure," and that "by the end of 1962 the spasm appeared to be over." The two sides

---

The Cold War as History, by Louis J. Halle. Harper and Row. 434 pp. $6.95.

---

were by no means ready to swear eternal friendship, but they were beginning to be ready to make peace, and Mr. Halle believes this peace will eventually be achieved "although its achievement would be delayed by all the repercussions of the American involvement in Asia."

He points out that heretofore such conflicts between powerful societies resulted finally in military conflict. Yet despite all of the shooting that has been going on, this ultimate conflict has not taken place. Here is his explanation:

Since 1945, however, the presence on the scene of weapons that could, presumably, destroy the greatest societies in one blow, had had a major inhibiting effect on this tendency. What was historically unique about the Cold War was the restraining influence of the new weapons, which had prevented a conflict on the grand scale from culminating in general war. In the new weapons, then, lay the hope of the world, no less than its peril, as it moved into an unknown future.

Cold comfort? Possibly. Yet perhaps a world which refrains from a new world war simply because it is so terrified by the thought of the catastrophe such a war would bring is, after all, beginning to learn something. In any case, here is a most provocative study of recent world history.

GO NOT IN SEARCH OF MONSTERS

Wherever the standard of freedom and independence has been unfurled, there will [America's] heart, her benedictions, and her prayers be. But she goes not abroad in search of monsters to destroy. She is the well-wisher to the freedom and independence of all. She is the champion and vindicator only of her own. She will recommend the general cause by the countenance of her voice and the benignant sympathy of her example. She well knows that, by once enlisting under other banners than her own, were they even the banners of foreign independence, she would involve herself, beyond the power of extrication, in all the wars of interest and intrigue, of individual avarice, envy, and ambition, which assume the color and usurp the standard of freedom. The fundamental maxims of her policy would insensibly change from liberty to force. The frontlet upon her brows would no longer beam with the ineffable splendor of freedom and independence; but in its stead would soon be substituted an imperial diadem, flashing in false and tarnished lustre the murky radiance of dominion and power. She might become the dictatress of the world; she would no longer be the ruler of her own spirit.

JOHN QUINCY ADAMS, *July 4, 1821*
Quoted in the Introduction to Twelve Against Empire

Monte Cassino CONTINUED FROM PAGE 23

ings were being used by the Germans and stated that in his opinion, if necessary, they should be blown down by artillery or bombardment."

Clark disagreed. The subject had been thoroughly discussed several weeks earlier, and American commanders felt that firing against the abbey was unwarranted. Civilians from the surrounding countryside were known to be taking shelter there. And the Americans doubted that enemy troops were using the building in any way. The Germans had no need of the abbey—the hill itself offered excellent sites for individual foxholes and for weapons emplacements, while higher hills nearby gave even better observation over the approaching Allied troops. What the Americans suspected was that the Germans would be glad to entice the Allies into bombing or shelling the building for the propaganda benefit to be gained. Moreover, the policy forbidding destruction of historical, religious, and cultural monuments was still in effect.

Yet the commander of the Indian division, General F. S. Tuker, a British officer, felt sure that the monastery was a very real obstacle to progress. He had closely studied the problem of taking Monte Cassino, and he had no illusions that the task would be easy. The strength of the enemy forces, the rugged terrain, and the freezing weather would make success extremely difficult. Symbolizing the advantages held by the Germans, and seeming to mock the Allied efforts, was the Benedictine monastery. Tuker felt that the abbey was exerting a baleful psychological influence on the Allied troops. He decided it would have to be destroyed in order to insure a successful attack with a minimum of losses. He therefore asked Freyberg for an air bombardment of the abbey.

Freyberg found himself in agreement with Tuker. He telephoned Clark. Clark was visiting the Anzio beachhead, and his chief of staff, General Gruenther, took the call. The time was 7 P.M., February 12.

"I desire that I be given air support tomorrow," Freyberg said, "in order to soften the enemy position in the Cassino area. I want three missions of twelve planes each; the planes to be Kitty Bombers carrying thousand-pound bombs."

The request was hardly excessive—thirty-six planes to drop eighteen tons of high explosive. Unfortunately, most of the planes in the theatre were scheduled to fly missions in support of the Anzio beachhead. Gruenther doubted that he could obtain thirty-six aircraft for the thirteenth, but said he would "go into the matter at once." After checking with his staff officers, he phoned the New Zealander and told him he could

have twelve A-36 fighter-bombers carrying 500-pound bombs for a single mission. Which target would he prefer the aircraft to attack?

"I want the convent attacked," Freyberg replied.

Did he mean the abbey of Monte Cassino?

"Yes," Freyberg said. "I want it bombed. The other targets are unimportant, but this one is vital. The division commander who is making the attack feels that it is an essential target, and I thoroughly agree."

The restrictions on that particular target, Gruenther said, made it impossible for him to approve the request. He would have to take up the matter with General Clark, and he promised to do so.

Unable to reach Clark for the moment, Gruenther telephoned General Alexander's chief of staff and explained the situation. He asked for Alexander's opinion as to "the advisability of authorizing the bombing." The chief of staff said he would talk with the General, and let Gruenther know.

Before the return call came, Gruenther reached General Clark, who said he saw no military necessity to destroy the monastery. Would Gruenther pass along his opinion to Alexander? Clark added that he felt somewhat embarrassed because of Freyberg's extremely strong views. If Clark refused an air bombardment and the Indian attack failed, he supposed he would be blamed for the failure.

Trying to marshal support for Clark's position, Gruenther next phoned General Geoffrey Keyes, the corps commander who was responsible for the American effort in the Cassino area. Keyes expressed his belief that there was no military necessity to destroy the monastery. He said further that bombing the monastery would "probably enhance its value as a military obstacle, because the Germans would then feel free to use it as a barricade."

Several minutes later—it was now 9:30 P.M.—Gruenther heard from Alexander's chief of staff. General Alexander had decided that the monastery should be bombed if Freyberg considered its reduction a military necessity. Alexander regretted "that the building should be destroyed, but he has faith in General Freyberg's judgment."

The announcement seemed final, but Gruenther tried to argue. He said that he had talked with General Clark since his earlier phone call. Clark's view was clear—he was against a bombing, so much so that if Freyberg were an American, Clark would turn him down. But "in view of General Freyberg's position in the British Empire forces, the situation was a delicate one, and General Clark hesitated to give him such an order without first referring the matter to General Alexander." Clark emphasized that a bombardment would endanger the lives of civilian refugees in the building, and that it very probably would enhance the value of the monastery as a defensive fortification.

The response was quite cold. "General Alexander," his chief of staff said, "has made his position quite clear. . . . He regrets very much that the monastery should be destroyed, but he sees no other choice."

Gruenther now phoned Clark again and reported Alexander's reaction. Somewhat upset, Clark asked Gruenther to tell Freyberg that he, Clark, "was willing to defer to General Freyberg's judgment." At the same time, he wanted Gruenther to tell Alexander that Clark would speak personally with him in the morning in order to state fully his conviction that bombing the monastery would be an error. Meanwhile, Gruenther was to go ahead and set up the bombing mission —but to schedule it for no earlier than 10 A.M. By that time, Clark hoped to have spoken with Alexander; if Alexander changed his mind, the bombardment could still be cancelled.

Gruenther first passed Clark's message on to Alexander's chief of staff; then—at 10 P.M.—he telephoned Freyberg once more to say that he was "reluctant to authorize [the abbey's] bombing unless you are certain that its destruction is necessary."

Freyberg refused to budge. It was not "sound," he said, "to give an order to capture Monastery Hill [Monte Cassino] and at the same time deny the commander the right to remove an important obstacle to the success of this mission." A higher commander who refused to authorize the bombing, he warned, would have to be held responsible if the attack failed.

Gruenther repeated that Clark was ready to authorize the bombing if Freyberg considered it a military necessity.

Yes, Freyberg said; in his "considered opinion," the bombardment was "a military necessity."

The magic formula having been categorically stated, Gruenther informed him that the air mission was authorized. Would he please arrange to move any Allied troops who might be endangered by the bombing to a safe place?

Around midnight, Freyberg called back. Would Gruenther temporarily defer the bombardment? There was not time to move the Allied troops to safety.

For the moment, the unpleasant prospect of destroying the monastery was averted.

On the morning of February 13, Clark talked on the telephone with Alexander and told him that he was "greatly concerned." Despite Freyberg's conviction

that the Germans were using the abbey for military purposes, there was no firm proof. But they would certainly have no compunctions about using it after a bombing. Humanitarian, religious, and sentimental reasons, Clark said, also argued against bombing. There was in addition a practical problem—the number of aircraft available to attack the building would be unable to destroy the value of the structure as a defensive work. These considerations, he felt, were more valid than the slim chance of facilitating the capture of the mountain.

All this was so, Alexander admitted. But if Freyberg wanted the monastery bombed, the monastery would have to be bombed.

Yet despite his apparent assurance, Alexander referred the matter to his immediate superior, Field Marshal Sir Henry Maitland Wilson, a British officer who had succeeded Eisenhower in command of the Mediterranean theatre. Wilson approved Alexander's view—what Freyberg wanted he would have to have.

Facing the massive force of Freyberg's personality and prestige, all his superiors were uncomfortable. It seemed unlikely that the Germans had violated the sanctity of the abbey. Yet it was true that some of their positions were so close that it was scarcely possible to fire on them without striking the religious structure.

It was true also that many soldiers sincerely believed that the Germans *were* using the building for military purposes. One regimental commander thought he had seen the flash of field glasses within the monastery. An Italian civilian declared that he had counted eighty

Bill Mauldin, the famous World War II cartoonist, vividly clarified the predicament of American troops on the Anzio beachhead by having two tired "dogfaces" look back at it after they finally took the heights the Germans had held.

"My God! Here they wuz an' there we wuz."

BOTH DRAWINGS © 1944 BY UNITED FEATURE SYNDICATE, INC.; REPUBLISHED BY COURTESY OF BILL MAULDIN.

Mauldin's cartoon of American infantrymen fighting in the craggy mountains of Italy, although generalized, indicates one reason for the heavy casualties in the ground assault on Monte Cassino in January, 1944: when the German guns opened fire, there wasn't any dirt for the G.I.'s to hit.

"Hit th' dirt, boys!"

Germans manning thirty machine guns inside the building. An American artillery battalion reported that "our observers had noted a great deal of enemy activity in the vicinity of the famous monastery, and it became ever clearer that they were using the abbey as an observation post and also had gun emplacements installed." A rifleman had been seriously wounded "by a sniper," he said, "hiding in the monastery." And frequent reports verified "much small arms fire seen and heard coming from the vicinity of the abbey."

To settle the question of whether German troops were actually inside the abbey, General Jacob Devers, Wilson's American deputy, and General Ira Eaker, the American in command of the Mediterranean theatre air forces, flew over the German lines in two small observation planes. Because the Germans rarely fired on light aircraft, which they suspected were sometimes decoys sent up to draw fire and pinpoint the location of their guns, Generals Devers and Eaker were able to pass directly above the abbey. Both believed they saw radio masts inside the monastery walls, and other convincing proof of the presence of enemy soldiers.

This confirmed the military necessity of a bombardment. In a report made later to explain his approval of the act, Field Marshal Wilson said he had what he called "irrefutable evidence" that the abbey was part of the German main line of defense, that observers were directing artillery fire from within the building, that snipers fired from the structure, and that gun emplacements, pillboxes, and ammunition dumps were located within the shadow of the walls. Thus, when General Freyberg insisted that destroying the abbey was a necessary preliminary for taking Monte Cassino, his argument, Wilson said, outweighed "historical and sentimental considerations."

The ground attack of the New Zealand and Indian divisions having been postponed to February 15, a bombardment was scheduled for the same day. But this bombing was to be far different from Freyberg's original request. No longer was he talking of a few planes attacking to soften the defenses. He was now saying that the abbey would have to be flattened before the Indians could take the mountain.

What had caused the escalation? There was a growing concern over the security of the Anzio beachhead, where the precarious equilibrium between Allied and German forces seemed about to tip in favor of the Germans—who, as it turned out, actually launched a massive attack on the sixteenth. There was an uneasy feeling that time was slipping by—that the cross-Channel attack was fast approaching while Rome remained as distant and elusive as ever. There was an increasing realization that some extraordinary measure was needed to blast through the Cassino defenses. And there was an idea novel to the doctrine of warfare, and as yet untried: that the power of massed strategic bombers, normally used for long-range missions, might contribute to a tactical victory—which would give the employment of heavy bombers at Monte Cassino the additional dimension of an experiment.

Still, the military debate was not over. The ranking French commander in Italy, General Alphonse Juin, made a special trip to see Clark on the fourteenth to urge that the abbey not be destroyed. Christendom, he said, would be shocked. Clark agreed with that judgment; but unfortunately, he said, the decision was irrevocable.

That evening, Allied planes dropped leaflets on Monte Cassino to warn the civilians in the vicinity of the impending bombardment. Apparently none fell within the walls of the abbey. A refugee—at some danger to himself, for there was firing all around— emerged from the building and retrieved one. He took it to the Abbot.

"Italian friends," the leaflet read. "Until this day we have done everything to avoid bombing the abbey. But the Germans have taken advantage. Now that the battle has come close to your sacred walls we shall, despite our wish, have to direct our arms against the monastery. Abandon it at once. Put yourselves in a safe place. Our warning is urgent." The message was signed "Fifth Army."

The Abbot sent his secretary to a nearby German headquarters to make arrangements for the occupants to leave. By the time he arrived, it was late; too late, the Germans said, for the inhabitants of the abbey to depart that night. They could guarantee the safety of the civilians only during the hours of darkness. Since daylight of the fifteenth would soon come, they recommended deferring the evacuation until the following night. The Abbot agreed, promising to have everyone ready to leave just before dawn of the sixteenth.

On the morning of February 15, about 250 Allied bombers attacked the monastery. According to one observer, they "soon reduced the entire top of Monte Cassino to a smoking mass of rubble." The planes attacked in waves, dropping about 600 tons of high explosive. Soldiers on a neighboring slope watched in awe. Between the waves of bombers, allied artillery fired on the target, adding to the destruction.

The attack seemed to confirm the presence of Germans in the abbey. "Over 150 enemy were seen wildly trying to get away from the Abbey as the first planes dropped their loads," one observer reported. "Artillery and small arms fire took a heavy toll of these men as they exposed themselves across the open terrain." Other witnesses thought they saw German troops make repeated attempts to dash from the abbey to safer positions, "conclusive proof," one said, "that the Germans had used the monastery for military purposes."

Brigadier General Frank Allen, head of the 1st Armored Division's Combat Command B, found the sight inspiring. "Our air," he wrote, "thoroughly demolished the monastery above Cassino. Reports indicate that a great number of Germans were driven out of the building and surrounding area. It was a tremendous spectacle to see all the Flying Fortresses come over and drop their bombs."

But Major General Fred L. Walker, who commanded the 36th Division, felt quite otherwise. "This was a valuable historical monument," he wrote, "which should have been preserved. The Germans were not using it and I can see no advantage in destroying it. No tactical advance will result since the Germans can make as much use of the rubble for observation posts and gun positions as of the building itself. Whether the Germans used the building for an observation post or for emplacements makes little difference since the mountain top on which the building stands can serve the same purpose. If I had had the decision to make I would have prevented its destruction. I have directed my artillery not to fire on it to date."

Yet to many Americans who had unsuccessfully assaulted Monte Cassino without benefit of this kind of air support, and who had suffered a psychological malaise from the hypnotic effect of the building, the immediate reaction was merely one of bitterness. Why had *they* been denied this assistance?

The assistance, however, proved futile. Though airplanes returned on the afternoon of the fifteenth to hammer again at the ruined abbey, though 150 aircraft struck on the following day, and fifty-nine on the seventeenth, though artillery expended an enormous number of shells directly against the abbey, the Indians failed to take the hill and the New Zealanders failed to force a passage across the Rapido. For the time being, the military situation at Cassino remained unchanged. The beachhead at Anzio was still isolated.

Aside from the destruction of the abbey, the bombardment blasted and burned off much of the vegetation on Monte Cassino. Stripped of its cover, the hill revealed a surprising complex of dugouts and trenches, thus confirming, in the words of one report, its "extensive organization . . . by the enemy."

Around noon of February 15, the German corps commander in the Cassino sector, General Frido von Senger und Etterlin, had informed Vietinghoff of the bombardment. Senger was calm and confident. "Field police," he reported, "have maintained steady watch that no German soldier entered the building. Therefore, the enemy measures lack any legal basis."

Ten years after the war, Senger firmly repeated that no German troops were inside the abbey before the bombardment. He confirmed Clark's view: there was no need to use the abbey as an observation post, because other sites on the mountain offered better locations. Anxious to keep from alienating the good will of the Vatican and of Catholics throughout the world, the Germans were scrupulous in respecting the neutrality of the monastery; so scrupulous, in fact, Senger said, that when he visited the abbey on Christmas eve of 1943 and dined with the Abbot, he was careful not to abuse the privilege. He refrained from looking out of the windows. Yet he admitted that observation posts and weapons were "as close as 200 yards" from the abbey walls.

A civilian who had been in the abbey during the bombardment and who came into the American lines on the following day confirmed that the Germans had never had weapons inside the abbey and had never used it as an observation post. Numerous emplacements, he added, were no more than two hundred yards from the outside wall, and one position was about fifty yards away.

Ten days after the bombardment, Fifth Army counterintelligence agents verified the fact that no German troops had occupied the abbey before the bombardment. But the information was given no dissemination. The Allied forces never officially announced whether German troops had been in the monastery.

One thing soon became self-evident: the Germans had little hesitation about moving in afterward. They waited exactly two days. Then, when the Abbot departed, German paratroopers installed themselves and their weapons in the ruins. The rubble provided excellent protection against the attacks on the mountain by the Indians.

On the day after the bombardment, German photographers took pictures of the destroyed monastery. That evening an officer flew the films to Berlin for processing. They would receive wide showing and have great propaganda effect. This, the Nazi Ministry of Information would proclaim, was how the Allies were liberating Europe.

Abbot Diamare left the ruined monastery at dawn on February 17. He and most of the other occupants had huddled in the deep crypt of the abbey during the bombardment. Now, accompanied by those who could walk, he wended his way down a mule path until he was picked up by Senger's automobile, which had been solicitously dispatched to bring him to the German's headquarters. Brokenhearted, dazed by the shock of the bombs, hardly believing what had happened, the Abbot accepted Senger's hospitality.

After letting him rest a day, Senger interviewed the Abbot in front of microphones. The production started with a statement read by a lieutenant:

The Abbey Monte Cassino is completely destroyed. A senseless act of force of the Anglo-American Air Force has robbed civilized mankind of one of its most valued cultural monuments. Abbot Bishop Gregorio Diamare has been brought out of the ruins of his abbey under the protection of the German Armed Forces. He voluntarily placed himself in their protection and was brought by them through a ring of fire of Allied artillery . . . and into the Command Post of the Commanding General. The aged Abbot . . . found here a place of refuge and recovery after the days of horror which he, his monks, and numerous refugees, women, children, old men, crippled, sick and wounded civilians had to undergo because of the order of the Allied Supreme Commander.

We find the General . . . and the Abbot . . . in a voluntary discussion into which we now cut in:

The General: ". . . everything was done on the part of the German Armed Forces, definitely everything, in order to give the opponent no military ground for attacking the monastery."

The Abbot: "General, I . . . can only confirm this. You declared the Abbey Monte Cassino a protected zone, you forbade German soldiers to step within the area of the abbey, you ordered that within a specified perimeter around the abbey there be neither weapons, nor observation posts, nor billeting of troops. You have tirelessly taken care that these orders were most strictly observed. . . . Until the moment of the destruction . . . there was within the area of the abbey neither a German soldier, nor any German weapon, nor any German military installation."

The General: "It came to my attention much too late that leaflets which gave notice of the bombing were dropped over the area of the monastery. I first learned this after the bombing. No leaflets were dropped over our German positions."

The Abbot: "I have the feeling that the leaflets were intionally dropped so late in order to give us no possibility to notify the German commander, or, on the other hand to bring the some eight hundred guests of the monastery out of the danger zone. . . . We simply did not believe that the English and Americans would attack the abbey. And when they came with their bombs, we laid out white cloths in order to say to them, do nothing to us, we are certainly without arms, we are no military objective, here is a holy place. It did not help, they have destroyed the monastery and killed hundreds of innocent people."

The General: "Can I do anything more?"

The Abbot: "No, General, you have done everything—even

AN AFTERWORD:

Lieutenant General Ira C. Eaker was Commander in Chief of the Mediterranean Allied Air Forces in 1944; consequently the mission against the abbey of Monte Cassino was carried out by his bombers. One of America's most distinguished airmen, General Eaker was chief pilot of the famous Army Air Force plane *Question Mark*, which in 1929 set an endurance record of over six days and nights; in 1936 he made the first transcontinental "blind" flight, using instruments only. Soon after America's entry into World War II he became commander of the Eighth Air Force, in England; from 1945 until his retirement in 1947, he was Deputy Chief of Staff of the United States Army Air Forces. Co-author with General Henry H. Arnold of several books on air power, he currently writes a syndicated newspaper column on aviation and military matters.

AMERICAN HERITAGE asked General Eaker to comment on Mr. Blumenson's article, and he has replied as follows:

"Whether the Germans were actually inside the Monte Cassino monastery is immaterial, since they did in fact occupy and fortify the mountain surrounding the monastery. Any serious attempt to deny them this vital observation and communications high ground, either with bombs or artillery, would have been impossible without severe damage to the abbey.

"When General Devers and I flew over Monte Cassino we clearly identified German soldiers and their radio masts. I could have dropped my binoculars into machine-gun nests less than fifty feet from the walls of the ancient building.

"If Mr. Blumenson means to imply that I opposed the bombing of Monte Cassino, he is only partly right. I did recommend against the use of medium and heavy bombers, believing fighter bombers with light bombs and smoke could achieve the military purpose. I believed then as now that it is the duty of every commander to reduce his casualties to the minimum, and I fully agreed that failure to deny Monte Cassino to the enemy would mean intoday the German Armed Forces provides for us and for the refugees in model fashion. But I have something still to do, namely to thank you and the German Armed Forces for all the consideration given to the original abode of the Benedictine Order both before and after the bombardment. I thank you."

Senger must have thanked the Abbot, although this was not recorded. He sent him under escort to Rome.

The Vatican protested the bombardment in strong terms, and President Roosevelt replied that he had issued instructions to prevent the destruction of historic monuments except in cases of military necessity —not merely military convenience, he emphasized, but military necessity. The bombardment, he said, had been unfortunate but necessary for the prosecution of the war.

In the Allied camp, a profound disappointment took hold. Who had been at fault? The Army troops who had failed to take advantage of the bombing? Or the airmen who had failed to eradicate the enemy defenses? Was heavy bombing useless for giving direct support to troops on the ground?

No one seemed to know. General Eaker, the air forces commander, summed up the feeling: General Clark, he wrote, "did not want a single bomb on Cassino Abbey, but . . . General Freyberg . . . went over his head or around him and asked . . . [Alexander] to have it bombed. We bomb it and it causes an uproar from the churchmen. You ask us then why we bombed; we make an investigation and discover a difference of view."

Exactly a month later, on March 15, the Allies launched another bombardment. This one employed twice as many planes as before, and the target was the town of Cassino. Although nearly all of its homes and buildings were destroyed, German paratroopers fought stubbornly amidst the ruins, and Allied ground attacks were only partly successful. Meanwhile, the wreckage of the monastery, high above the battle, remained in German hands.

At Anzio, the isolated Allied troops withstood German pressure by sheer determination, a scant seven miles from the water's edge. A virtual stalemate then characterized the military situation in Italy until early in May, when the Allies launched an overwhelming attack along the Cassino line. Clark's Fifth Army, spearheaded by Juin's French forces, broke the Cassino defenses at the Garigliano River, outflanked Monte Cassino, and forced the Germans to give way. Polish troops then captured what was left of the abbey. Toward the end of May, after moving forward relentlessly, American forces made contact with the troops at Anzio, who then broke out of their confined beachhead. A subsequent drive resulted in the capture of Rome on June 4, two days before the Normandy invasion.

Almost immediately after the battlefront had swept past Monte Cassino, plans were made to rebuild the abbey. And soon after the end of World War II, sufficient funds were raised throughout the world, with a large part coming from the United States, to start the laborious process of restoration.

Today Saint Benedict's structure again occupies its mountaintop serenely, a landmark visible from afar. Tourists speeding along the new superhighway between Naples and Rome can look across the fields and see it plainly in all its glory. There are no scars. Who can imagine that anything happened to the abbey during the war?

Martin Blumenson, formerly with the Army's Office of the Chief of Military History, is now a free-lance writer in Washington, D.C. He is the author of The Duel for France; Anzio: The Gamble that Failed; *and* Kasserine Pass.

---

creased Allied casualties. Under my proposal, the abbey undoubtedly would have been damaged, but not reduced to rubble.

"It should be added that Monte Cassino did not prove that strategic bombers could never be usefully employed in support of ground troops. It is true that the destruction of the abbey failed to break the German line on February 15. Nor was a similar aerial bombardment of the town of Cassino itself, at the foot of the mountain, successful in providing a break-through for the ground forces a month later. But the lessons we learned from those two attacks provided invaluable guidance for the invasion of Normandy in June, when such saturation bombings of enemy front-line positions proved highly effective.

"The author has overdrawn considerably, I believe, the propaganda effect of our Monte Cassino bombing. At any rate, the Germans did not deliberately induce us to bomb the abbey in order to obtain a propaganda advantage. They needed the mountaintop for military reasons, since we had gained complete air superiority and they could not use observation planes.

"Soon after Allied troops occupied Rome, our Vatican representative, Mr. Myron Taylor, suggested and arranged an audience for me with Pope Pius XII. When I expressed regret about the bombing of Monte Cassino, but explained its significance as a military target, the pontiff seemed to understand fully. He commended the obvious effort our air forces had made to avoid destruction of historical and religious monuments elsewhere, and referred particularly to our bombing of Rome's railway yards without inflicting civilian casualties or damaging Roman antiquities.

"Italy is the world's greatest jewel box of art and architectural treasures. To me, it is a miracle of the Italian campaign—and a great tribute to the carefulness of the Allied commanders —that there was so little damage. Had there been more damage to historic places, perhaps the story of the Cassino abbey would not stand out so prominently."

The Slopes of Kilimanjaro

CONTINUED FROM PAGE 43

a direct quotation from Madame Marie Rohrbach, who was in service to Ernest and Hadley during most of their time in Paris.

There is also a reminiscence of a fishing vacation in the Black Forest of Germany in August, 1922. Hemingway romanticizes and fictionizes his trip to Constantinople and Adrianople to cover the Greco-Turkish War as correspondent for the Toronto *Star*. He also goes out of his way to insult the Left Bank literati by retailing a trivial incident connected with Harry's homecoming from the Middle East. On the way back to his apartment the day of his return, Harry passes a café and glances inside. There sits "Malcolm Cowley with a pile of saucers in front of him and a stupid look on his face talking about the Dada movement with . . . Tristan Tzara." Hemingway deleted Cowley's name before the story appeared. Harry's wife forgives him for going to Constantinople, just as Hadley forgave Ernest that October morning in 1922, though she had refused to speak to him for three days before his departure because she was afraid to be left alone in the rough neighborhood of the rue du Cardinal Lemoine and the Place Contrescarpe. Hemingway seems to have invented the episode in which Harry's first wife dis-

> *And there in the café as he passed was that American poet with a pile of saucers in front of him and a stupid look on his potato face talking about the Dada movement with a Roumanian who said his name was Tristan Tzara, who always wore a monocle and had a headache, and, back at the apartment with his wife that now he loved again, the quarrel all over, the madness all over, glad to be home, the office sent his mail up to the flat. So then the letter in answer to the one he'd written came in on a platter one morning and when he saw the handwriting he went cold all over and tried to slip the letter underneath another. But his wife said, "Who is that letter from, dear?" and that was the end of the beginning of that.*

covers a love letter from another girl in the morning mail, though something not unlike this may have happened while Ernest was conducting a surreptitious liaison with Pauline Pfeiffer before she became his second wife.

The apartment in the rue Notre Dame des Champs, where Ernest, Hadley, and their infant son, John, lived after their return from Toronto, does not figure in this story because Hemingway had already used it in

> *There never was another part of Paris that he loved like that, the sprawling trees, the old white plastered houses painted brown below, the long green of the autobus in that round square, the purple flower dye upon the paving, the sudden drop down the hill of the rue Cardinal Lemoine to the River, and the other way the narrow crowded world of the rue Mouffetard. The street that ran up toward the Pantheon and the other that he always took with the bicycle, the only asphalted street in all that quarter, smooth under the tires, with the high narrow houses and the cheap tall hotel where Paul Verlaine had died. There were only two rooms in the apartments where they lived and he had a room on the top floor of that hotel that cost him sixty francs a month where he did his writing, and from it he could see the roofs and chimney pots and all the hills of Paris.*
>
> *From the apartment you could only see the wood and coal man's place. He sold wine too, bad wine. The golden horse's head outside the Boucherie Chevaline where the carcasses hung yellow gold and red in the open window, and the green painted co-operative where they bought their wine; good wine and cheap. The rest was plaster walls and the windows of the neighbors. The neighbors who, at night, when some one lay drunk in the street, moaning and groaning in that typical French ivresse that you were propaganded to believe did not exist, would open their windows and then the murmur of talk.*
>
> *"Where is the policeman? When you don't want him the bugger is always there. He's sleeping with some concierge. Get the Agent." Till some one threw a bucket of water from a window and the moaning stopped. "What's that? Water. Ah, that's intelligent." And the windows shutting. Marie, his femme de menage, protesting against the eight-hour day saying, "If a husband works until six he gets only a little drunk on the way home and does not waste too much. If he works only until five he is drunk every night and one has no money. It is the wife of the working man who suffers from this shortening of hours."*

a flashback in *Green Hills of Africa*. But it was from this apartment, in the early winters of 1924–25 and 1925–26, that the Hemingways twice left for the village of Schruns in the Austrian Vorarlberg so that Ernest could write and ski in comparative peace. Harry is made to recall the village and to use the actual name of Walther Lent, who operated a ski school in Schruns and played poker with Ernest at the Madlenerhaus, an Alpine hut high in the Silvretta Range. Another of Hemingway's favorite locales which comes into Harry's mind is the valley of the Clarks Fork branch of the Yellowstone River in Wyoming. Harry is made to remember "the silvered gray of the sage brush, the quick, clear water in the irrigation ditches, and the heavy green of the alfalfa." The violent anecdote of the half-wit chore boy who murdered his cantankerous employer is largely though not entirely an invention of Hemingway's, based on a real-life story dating from 1912 that he had overheard during one of his visits to Wyoming. This brings to an end the pastiche of truth and fiction which courses through Harry's memory as he lies dying, full of vain regret that he has not used enough of what he knows in what he has written.

For the climactic scene of his story, Hemingway drew upon yet another autobiographical episode. Though actually on the very brink of death, Harry is made to imagine that an airplane has arrived to carry him back to the hospital in Nairobi. Hemingway was flown out of the plains country to Nairobi on January 16, 1934, in a Puss Moth biplane for treatment of a severe case of amoebic dysentery. Harry recalls in detail the arrival of the plane, the appearance of the bush pilot, the look of the land, and the behavior of the grazing animals as the plane takes off for the long flight to the north, passing on the way the enormous snow-capped western summit of Kilimanjaro. This was where the adventurous leopard had succumbed to the altitude, only to lie preserved forever in his "meta-physical" fastness. But Harry has died without having attained a similar height.

One of Hemingway's recurrent motivations to literary creativity throughout his life was the conviction that he might soon be going to die without having completed his work or fulfilled his unwritten promise to his talents. At the time when he wrote this story he knew very well that he had climbed no farther than

> *In Schrunz, on Christmas day, the snow was so bright it hurt your eyes when you looked out from the weinstube and saw every one coming home from church. That was where they walked up the sleigh-smoothed urine-yellowed road along the river with the steep pine hills, skis heavy on the shoulder, and where they ran that great run down the glacier above the Madlener-haus, the snow as smooth to see as cake frosting and as light as powder and he remembered the noiseless rush the speed made as you dropped down like a bird.*
>
> *They were snow-bound a week in the Madlener-haus that time in the blizzard playing cards in the smoke by the lantern light and the stakes were higher all the time as Herr Lent lost more. Finally he lost it all. Everything, the skischule money and all the season's profit and then his capital. He could see him with his long nose, picking up the cards and then opening, "Sans Voir." There was always gambling then. When there was no snow you gambled and when there was too much you gambled. He thought of all the time in his life he had spent gambling.*

the lower slopes of his personal Kilimanjaro. It is at least a legitimate speculation that he read the passage in Vivienne de Watteville in a symbolic as well as a literal sense. Certainly he must have been struck by the statement that success depended "on one's ability to withstand the high altitude" as well as the warning that the attempt must be made "soon, before there was any risk of the rains setting in" to destroy his plans. This was one of the things he knew but felt "no obligation to tell" as he stood poised upon the slopes of the mountain in the midst of his career.

Mr. Baker, who is Woodrow Wilson Professor of Literature at Princeton, has adapted his article from an earlier version that appeared in the Fall, 1967, issue of Novel, *a new journal published at Brown University. His* Ernest Hemingway: A Life Story *will be published early in 1969 by Charles Scribner's Sons, who have authorized both the accompanying quotations from "The Snows of Kilimanjaro" (copyright 1936 Ernest Hemingway; renewal copyright © 1964) and the woodcuts from* Green Hills of Africa *(copyright 1935 Charles Scribner's Sons; renewal copyright © 1963 Charles Scribner's Sons and Mary Hemingway).*

THE GREAT RACETRACK CAPER

CONTINUED FROM PAGE 27

reported a rumor that the syndicate would fly a balloon over Gravesend on each race day, with observers, operators, and a telegraph station in its basket. The poolsellers never actually used the balloon, but the strategy they did employ was perhaps even more spectacular.

At 3 A.M. on opening day, heavy wagons loaded with lumber, men, and tools rolled up to Sleight's Hotel. The lumber was carried to the hotel's cupola and the carpenters went to work. The *World* described their efforts:

No circus tent ever went up faster. Ten feet into the air, then a staircase and a landing. Ten feet higher, another staircase, another landing. Another ten feet, another staircase and landing. The carpenters paused for breath.

It was daylight now and the Dwyer forces rallied in a hurry. A group of carpenters set to work to raise the fence still higher. Ten feet more, and the huge structure began to tremble with the weight of the workers. A breeze blew in from the bay and the men's hats flew off. They climbed down, glad to be on earth again. They looked across at the Western Union tower.

"Give her another story," commanded the [tower] foreman. The carpenters hammered and knocked together another staircase and ten more feet of altitude. The tower was now forty-two feet above the cupola and its top platform seventy-seven feet from the ground.

Western Union installed four wires and a half dozen operators in the new tower, the *World* reported, and stationed a guard at the door. In the gamblers' camp an air of triumph prevailed. Peter De Lacy walked about "with a quiet smile and remarked that he was content." He magnanimously handed a ten-dollar bill to some Gravesend employees and told them to "go blow it" on pie and milk. Racing Man-

ager M. J. McKenna of Western Union "looked pleased," the *Sun* recounted, as did "Little Abe" Hummel of Howe & Hummel, lawyers for the Poolsellers Association. From Manhattan, reports were arriving that De Lacy's own poolroom was packed and that business was booming in all the betting places. Racing information was said to be coming in fine.

"The Brooklyn Jockey Club owns the racecourse," De Lacy declared, "and has the right to withhold its news if it can. But I don't think the effort will be a success. We need that information and we're bound to get it."

But Sleight's Hotel was so situated that, even from their tower, telegraphers could not see the track's finish line; in close races they had to guess the winners. Nor could they observe odds and scratches, which the management was now posting under the judge's stand. When Western Union offered twenty-five dollars to the first person to get the information for each race through to the hotel, racegoers having no connection with either the syndicate or the telegraph company began to fling rubber balls filled with racing data over the fences. But the patrolling Pinkertons foiled most of these efforts.

The detectives also increased their vigilance over those admitted to the track. One day they noticed a tall young man in a close-fitting gray coat behaving strangely near the betting ring. He would button and unbutton his coat, raise and lower his hat, hold his pink sporting sheet at various angles, mop his brow, and bow in different directions. Sure enough, he was signalling post odds to a man seated in a tree outside the grounds who was apparently cooling himself vigorously with a palm-leaf fan. Actually he too was signalling, in Morse code, to observers in the tower. At about that time, the *Sun* reported, a carrier pigeon fluttered out of the grandstand's second tier; catching sight of it, the crowd roared, "There it goes!" "There it goes!" Unfortunately, the message it bore had been insecurely fastened to its leg; as the bird circled overhead before streaking for its coop, the paper dropped into the paddock.

By the time the second day's racing began, telegraph lines had been strung from barns and trees, with sending stations on some flat-topped stumps. The syndicate was reportedly paying $100 a day to a farmer named Young for the use of his two big locust trees as observation posts.

That night the Jockey Club's carpenters increased the height of the fence that stood in front of Farmer Young's trees. Next day the telegraphers climbed still higher, and the Gravesend carpenters appeared with more lumber. Lowering his binoculars, the man in the nearest tree shouted down to his telegrapher, "The horses are going to the post for the second race, and the Dwyers are building another fence!"

The *World* reported that one tree sitter received his signals from a baby, in the care of the "most innocent-looking woman in the grandstand."

The woman did not look like a regular, and certainly the baby didn't. It was a golden-haired, chubby little thing. When its mother—or alleged mother—secured the scratches and betting odds for the second race, she went down to within a few feet of the track, spread her shawl upon the ground and proceeded to amuse the baby.

While the little one kicked its heels in the air, filled its little mouth with tiny fingers and said "goo-goo" the young woman waved a green parasol up and down before its delighted eyes. It didn't make any difference to the baby that each motion of the parasol was a Morse Code dot or dash. And Mr. Dwyer and Mr. Pinkerton stood twenty feet away at the judge's stand and didn't suspect a thing. This little by-play was repeated after the second and third races. Then the new fence and a rainstorm broke up the combination.

Meanwhile, at one entrance the gatemen were challenging a woman. One grabbed at her clothes and a pigeon squawked. "Why," said a detective, "she's got enough pigeons on her to stock a good-sized loft. That dress has pockets all the way down. We know too much about shop-lifters to be fooled by a game like that."

Nevertheless, the poolsellers' lawyers estimated that fully a hundred pigeons were smuggled into the track that day. The Jockey Club reportedly hired "Snapper" Garrison, an unemployed jockey with a reputation as a champion pigeon shot.

Despite such efforts, signallers continued to infest the grounds. Red, white, blue, yellow, and green handkerchiefs fluttered from many points. The Pinkertons hustled a half dozen men out the gate for twirling their mustaches and walking sticks in a "suspicious" manner. One of them charged that he had been degraded when paraded in custody before the grandstand, and announced that he would sue.

The track management further confounded the poolroom forces by concealing the names of entries until twenty minutes before post time for each race. A printer named Eagan was employed to run the information off on slips of paper, using a portable press set up at the track. "The crowd lay in wait for the messengers who distributed the slips and rushed upon them with much scrambling," the *Herald* reported.

Gradually, it seemed, the cops were beating the robbers. Conditions at the betting places in Manhattan were dismal. Crowds melted, and the bettors who did come complained loudly of the poor service. At De Lacy's own place, the announcer said at 2:42 P.M.,

"They're at the post at Brooklyn." It was thirty-two minutes later when he got the word, "They're off at Brooklyn!" One place had the horses running in the stretch for two minutes. Some betting rooms posted signs, "Not Responsible For Errors In Weights And Jockeys." All this encouraged the antigambling *Times* to headline its lead story: "POOL MEN BEATEN AT LAST."

But the poolroom forces had a few tricks left. The next afternoon a pole was set up near Gravesend's lower turn, its top poking above the fence like the head of a great serpent. A telegrapher climbed on spikes to the crossarm near the top, took off his hat, and bowed solemnly in the direction of President Dwyer's box. Then he hauled up a telegraph key and fastened it to the pole. "In three minutes," the *Herald* reported, "he had a little telegraph office in operation, ninety feet in the air. He was a facetious little man as well as a bold one. No sooner was his shop in order than he pulled a national flag from his pocket and nailed it bravely to the top of the pole."

That night workmen planted another pole in a yard east of the track. It stood 120 feet high. When its telegrapher reached the top the following day, he was greeted by his colleague atop the shorter pole on the lower turn, who snatched his flag from the mast and waved it around his head.

At this point, the Pinkertons began to raise their own poles within the grounds. Each carried a great spread of canvas, like the mast of a sailing ship, which effectively blocked the views from the poles outside. Even so, the pole sitters returned to their perches on the days that followed, although the Pinkertons were certain they could see nothing of value. Pigeons had been cleared from the grounds, ball-throwing had ceased, and no signallers were in sight.

Still there was a leak somewhere. "By some mysterious means," said the *World*, "whether by necromancy, juggling or what, the 'pool rooms' yesterday seemed in their normal condition. Betting was in full swing on all the events at Brooklyn. Jockeys, with the exception of the first race, were listed. No one seemed to know how the information from Brooklyn had been obtained."

Robert Pinkerton and his men managed to unravel the mystery before the fall meeting ended. What they discovered was proclaimed in these *World* headlines: "ELECTRICITY IN THE HAT. THE MOST INGENIOUS SCHEME YET FOR OBTAINING RACING NEWS."

"Every afternoon," the *Herald* explained the next day, a "handsome barouche, drawn by a pair of spirited horses, whirled a party of ladies and gentlemen to the lawn just above the betting ring. The driver parked his vehicle at a spot near the track, and the party seemingly turned themselves to enjoying a holiday. They had lunch and wine and cigars in plenty and seemed bent on nothing but enjoying the sweets of life...."

Had the Pinkertons scrutinized the barouche more carefully, they might have noticed that the coachman wore an unusually tall silk hat and that he kept his seat on the box while members of the party visited the betting ring or viewed the races. They returned to the carriage now and then, ostensibly to refresh themselves. This continued daily until five days before the season ended, when Pinkerton and his men raided the coach. The picnicking group was headed by Joseph W. Frost, an electrician and president of the Automatic Fire Alarm Company, 317 Broadway. He was accompanied by his wife, Eliza, and their ten-year-old son; Frost's brother, a onetime Indian agent and now manager of a Washington, D.C., hotel; a Mrs. C. A. LaVille; and the coachman, C. S. Pearsall, who, not entirely by coincidence, was a telegrapher.

It developed that Joseph Frost had arranged with the syndicate to supply complete racing information from Gravesend to Western Union for $1,000 a day, and he had succeeded in doing so for six days. Pearsall's tall coachman's hat had a hole in the center of its top the size of a half dollar. Inside the hat was a small electric light powered by batteries concealed in the coach. Under his clothing Pearsall wore a network of wires that connected the light with the batteries and with a telegraph key hidden on the coach floor.

Members of the party brought him information on odds, jockeys, and the like from the betting ring. The finishes Pearsall observed himself, simply by standing up in the carriage. He sent a running story by operating the key with his foot, causing the light in his hat to go on and off in Morse code. The telegraph operator in the hotel tower could not see the finish

line or the posted odds, but he had a fine view of the top of the coachman's hat. Somehow or other the Pinkertons were tipped off, and suddenly one afternoon Robert Pinkerton himself leaped into the carriage and dragged Frost from it. During the struggle, Mrs. Frost screamed, "Turn that man loose!" and hit Pinkerton (he said later) on the head with her parasol. She claimed that Pinkerton had grabbed her by the throat and choked her. As the party was led away, Frost bellowed, "You'll suffer for this, as I have the Western Union Telegraph Company and ten million dollars at my back." The bookmakers left their stands and shouted in excitement. Bettors abandoned the ring and shouted encouragement to the Frosts. One man jumped over the fence, snatched off his coat, and, directing his ire at the Pinkertons, yelled, "Come on and hang 'em!" The crowd in the ring shouted, "Lynch 'em!" "Lynch 'em!"

Fortunately, nobody was lynched, and the carriage episode became the final act of "the Great Battle of Gravesend" as public spectacle. Thereafter, De Lacy and his cohorts resorted to more subtle strategems.

By instituting or backing a number of lawsuits during the decade following 1891, De Lacy secured several lower court decisions holding the Ives Law unconstitutional. Since that law had declared that the only place a man could get down a legal bet was at a racetrack, these findings had the effect, temporarily, of making *all* betting a crime in the state. Thus, in 1893, De Lacy secured the arrest of Phil Dwyer, by then a millionaire who controlled most of the racing in the metropolitan area, but the charges were dismissed in the higher courts. Meanwhile, track managements were bringing pressure on the police to close the poolrooms. De Lacy's own place was closed in 1893, but at the turn of the century the tenacious "Poolroom King" was still plaguing racetrack managements with arrests and lawsuits.

The man who came close to wrecking thoroughbred racing in New York state was not De Lacy, however, but the reform governor—and future presidential candidate, Secretary of State, and Chief Justice—Charles Evans Hughes. His administration outlawed all racetrack betting, and that closed every established track in the state after the end of the 1910 season. But racing interests got this law repealed in time to resume in 1913, and the sport of kings has thrived ever since.

Not, however, in Brooklyn: old Gravesend Racetrack, which closed with the others, failed to re-open in 1913. Brooklyn was changing from a center of sport to a "city of homes," and the land was later sold for real-estate development.

In the past few years, urged on mainly by New York City, which hopes for increased tax revenues, some members of the state legislature have made serious attempts to legalize off-track betting. They have not succeeded to date, but the idea refuses to die. It is possible that after all this time Peter De Lacy may eventually win his point.

Mr. Jarman, formerly a staff member on The New Yorker *and the* Saturday Evening Post, *is an instructor at the Famous Writers School in Westport, Connecticut.*

editor of the *Outlook,* told Washington he not only could, but should, do better. Wide distribution of a better biographical reminiscence, Abbott told him, would "do good to the cause you have at heart." This time Washington wrote his story himself. He recorded his early life as he wanted the whole world to see it, and this is the version which has been uncritically accepted ever since.

The story started with a very human deception: Washington concealed his real age. It was understandable that he might be unsure, because many slaves did not really know exactly how old they were—and that was a point he wanted to make. Apparently, however, Washington did know. He had told his teachers at Hampton Institute in Virginia, where he went to school and later taught, that he was born in 1856, which was true. In 1899, when he was struggling with his first autobiography, he wrote to "correct" Hampton's record: "I am not sure of the year I was born, but recent investigations tend to show that it was about 1858 or 1859." In the same year, when he sent in his first entry to *Who's Who,* he made it "about 1859," thus admitting to forty rather than forty-three.

Forty as a male landmark was even more pronounced back in the nineties, in days of earlier mortality. He had been almost a prodigy, one of the youngest in his class at Hampton—so young that when in 1881 he was proposed as principal of Tuskegee the trustees didn't know whether to accept him. But now, in 1900, constant newspaper exposure had made it seem that Washington had been around for quite some time. He was even beginning to be called "the veteran leader." But probably more than personal pride was behind his concealment of his true age: he was constantly driven by a feeling that he had not yet done enough. As he said in the first paragraph of *The Story of My Life and Work:* "I hope that my life work, by reason of my present age, lies more in the future than in the past."

1856 was actually a vintage year. A number of babies were born in it who were to be heard from later— Sigmund Freud in Vienna; George Bernard Shaw in Dublin; and in Staunton, Virginia—not far away from Booker's birthplace—Thomas Woodrow Wilson. Unlike the other new arrivals, Booker had only one name. It was all that was required when his owner, James Burroughs, a planter near rural Halesford, Virginia, noted the birth in the family Bible and then rode over to the Rocky Mount courthouse and registered the birth of a child to his slave Jane, on April 5. Despite the fact that Booker was a common Virginia surname, used often for a first name, the clerk spelled

it Bowker at first. So did the man who recorded James Burroughs' estate when he died in 1861, by which time the baby had grown to be worth four hundred dollars.

The child was known as Burroughs' Booker. He was now a member of the close-knit household of a small rural slaveholder in which black and white worked together and considered themselves one family in a feudal sense. When the Burroughs daughters wrote to Washington years later they filled their chatty letters with news of all the relatives. At their best, little Booker's white owners were simple, direct, and kindly. He said that they were not "especially cruel . . . as compared with many others."

Yet there was always an undertow of force. In the plantation family the Negroes were the perpetual stepchildren, linked not only by law but by ties of dependence and enmity in an ambivalence that could not be resolved. For the Negro child, even after he grew up, was rarely allowed to leave. On this point, Washington did not want to be misunderstood. He wrote of the devotion some slaves felt for their masters, but he made it clear that he was not contributing to southern myth: "From some things I have said one may get the idea that some of the slaves did not want freedom. This is not true. I have never seen one who did not want to be free, nor one who would return to slavery."

The Burroughs family, like many other slaveholders, were slaves themselves in a sense, bound to a system that made them unkind without thinking. Little Booker was born on the packed dirt floor of a ramshackle cabin because that was the way things were in back-country Virginia in the 1850's. His white owners lived far from luxuriously. James Burroughs owned approximately two hundred acres in the poorer section of Franklin County, and he did not have a grand "Big House" with Greek Revival pillars. Like most Big Houses, his was large mainly in contrast to "the Quarters"—an elaborate term for the plantation's two slave cabins. Riders jolting down the Burroughs lane from the pike would have seen the house as the small-porched center of a cluster of outbuildings, dwarfed by a large barn on the right. The house had originally been only a two-room log cabin; an ell, a back porch, and a half-storied second floor had been added. The kitchen shack was behind the house, and it was there that Jane, as plantation cook, lived with her children.

Booker's home for nine years was a windowless room, about twelve by sixteen feet, with a big fireplace at one end. In the humid summers the heat seemed unbearable; in the winters the ill-fitting door and the cracks in the wall let in the cold. The beds were "pallets" that were rearranged every night from rags in the corner. Jane's children had all been born there. Booker and his older brother, John, were fathered by different white men; his little sister, Amanda, by Jane's slave husband. This, too, was the way things were in slavery, but on this plantation there was conscious guilt about it. James Burroughs' father was a Baptist preacher and this was a religious family.

White people lowered their voices when they discussed the parentage of mulatto slaves, and the very verbs they used were indicative of uneasiness. When it came to Jane's first child, John, they "blamed" Ben Burroughs, second son of Jane's master. When it came to Booker, they "accused" one of the Fergusons.

The identity of his father was one secret Washington never divulged. In *Up From Slavery* he wrote him off: "I do not even know his name. I have heard reports to the effect that he was a white man who lived on one of the nearby plantations. Whoever he was, I never heard of his taking the least interest in me, or providing in any way for my rearing."

Even his mulatto relative Biah Ferguson, when she accused Washington of not telling the whole truth, could not have wanted him to name his father. Not only the whites but the Negroes who absorbed their

The main building at Hampton Institute, Hampton, Virginia, where Washington taught before he founded Tuskegee

attitudes felt shame as well as anger about their sexual exploitation. The majority of slave women yielded to white men with the docility of despair—and then were considered immoral by white society. Biah herself was the illegitimate child of a slave named Mary Ann and her master—a planter named Josiah Ferguson, who lived in a handsome brick house across the pike from the Burroughs plantation. When people asked Biah why she didn't claim her relationship with Washington when he became famous, she said simply, "when you talk about that, you're talking about my mother."

This could also have been the reason that Washington, who adored his mother, dismissed the topic as briefly as he could. But certainly he could not help knowing he was a Ferguson. He looked like the white Ferguson family and very much like Biah and her little brothers and sisters across the road. Like them he had large gray eyes, so startling in a brown face as to look almost luminous. Probably he also knew exactly which one of the large Ferguson family was his father. All the evidence points to Josiah Ferguson's second eldest son, a brilliant, unreliable charmer named Thomas Benjamin Ferguson.

Ben, as he was called, was said to be "the brightest Ferguson that ever had that name." He was a twenty-five-year-old bachelor when his presumed son, Booker, was born. By the time Jane's baby was four Ben had moved away from the family and was in business for himself. He had a tobacco factory three miles down the pike near the post office of Taylor's Store, but his operation was unimpressive compared to the factory run by his industrious older brother, John Cardwell Ferguson, down at Halesford. When Ben enlisted in the Franklin Rangers—in the very first muster of May, 1861—the family finally had cause for pride in him.

The brave start did not last. At the end of his first year, he re-enlisted for only one year, in contrast with most of the company, who volunteered for "two years or the war." Shortly afterward he came down with varioloid—a light case of smallpox—but he recovered sufficiently so that he was judged fit to return to his company. He had married at some time in that first war year. His new wife was a schoolteacher with a long name (Angelina Florentina Thomas Wright Turner) and a small inheritance. He hired a susbstitute to rejoin the troop—a practice far more common in the North than in the South—and the substitute deserted in January of 1863. This must have been the last straw. Bright or not, Ben was the Ferguson black sheep.

Booker Washington had neither of the two reasons a mulatto might have to talk about his white blood. He was not one of those lucky few with an acknowledged and responsible father who had actually behaved as one—and they did exist—nor had his father been a man of particular prestige. Washington's reticence on the subject was so great that his own children were not sure who their white grandfather had been. Washington even helped create the illusion that he might have been someone else's son. When he was in his teens he started using the middle name of Taliaferro—long after he had chosen Washington as a last name. His explanation was that he had just discovered that his mother had given him this middle name when he was born. She might have done so. There was no one who commanded more respect in Franklin County when

Hampton was a normal and agricultural school, situated on fertile land whose tillage provided both training and sustenance for the students. Although Tuskegee's soil was poor, Washington instituted there the same dual-purpose program.

Booker was a little boy than old Dr. Richard McCulloch Taliaferro. The first practicing physician in the county seat of Rocky Mount, he also had a country place near Halesford. The name was pronounced Tolliver—and throughout the family-conscious South it was considered one of gentility rather than of simple yeomanry. Every slaveholder was automatically considered a member of the ruling class, but some were more ruling than others.

During slavery, Negroes absorbed white social distinctions easily and were proud of connections with an important family. After slavery, a small mulatto elite kept the pride alive, and when people assumed Booker Washington had Taliaferro blood, he did not deny it.

Neither did he deny that he was Ben Ferguson's son when it was printed in a newspaper in 1908, although Ferguson was the one name that Washington could not stand. It was not only the name of the white father who in the old days had given him no cause for pride. It was, by coincidence, the name of his Negro stepfather, Washington Ferguson, whom he actively resented. The resentment was stronger after freedom, because during slavery he rarely saw his stepfather. "Wash" Ferguson belonged to Josiah Ferguson, but he had been hired out to work on a railroad in western Virginia. He got home mostly at Christmastime—the universal holiday for everybody. His small stepson used to wonder "why he was so much interested in the building of a railroad that he could remain away from home for five or six months . . . at one time."

One Christmas Wash did not come home at all, and the whisper among the whites was that he had "gone off with the northern people." It was easy to do. Confederate troops were no longer in western Virginia after 1861, and two years later the territory pledged a gradual emancipation of the slaves within its borders when it applied to the Union for admission as a new state called West Virginia.

If Wash's failure to return was legal desertion in the minds of his owners, it was emotional desertion to his little stepson, who now had no semblance of a father, white or black. The only older man of his own race for him to look up to was his mother's half-brother, known on the Burroughs plantation as Uncle *Mon*roe. And Washington learned early the powerlessness of the Negro man—something more shocking than absence. He said afterward that nothing about slavery was as vivid to him as that morning when he saw his uncle, "a grown man tied to a tree, stripped naked and someone whipping him with a cowhide. As each blow touched his back, the cry 'Pray, Master! Pray, Master!' came from his lips." It was a memory which he said he would carry with him to his grave—but he did not choose to remember it in *Up From Slavery*.

If the Negro males in Washington's background were either absent or powerless, his mother, Jane, was there with the strength of ten. Although worn down physically, she was devoted and courageous. Washington was never able to find out much about her ancestry, but that didn't matter. "If I have done anything in life worth attention," he wrote, "I feel sure that I inherited the disposition from my mother." Her white owners valued her despite the fact that she was—in slavery's brutal phrase—"not a breeder" and worth only fifty dollars more on the market than her baby, Amanda. Laura Burroughs remembered that she was "more clever and intelligent than the average colored girl and was kept about the house on that account. She was an extra good cook, a particularly good ironer" who was "delighted to have her white people appear well." She was also sweet-tempered and forgiving. Yet the first knowledge little Booker had that he was a slave came one troubling morning when he was awakened by his mother's voice, nakedly fervent as he had rarely heard it. She was kneeling by him and his sleeping brother and baby sister, praying for Lincoln and the victory of his armies so that she and her children could go free.

Vivid memories of his mother were all of happenings at night or in the early morning, around the edges of the daylight hours during which, of course, her time and energy belonged to her owners. She and her children never sat down to a meal together. For them, it was "a piece of bread here and a scrap of bread there . . . gotten very much as animals get theirs." In a sense, the farm animals were better off: at least they had scheduled feeding times. In the morning, when the Indian corn was boiled for them, Booker used to get some before it went to the cows and pigs, or if he were too late, he could still find enough corn scattered around the fence or the trough. Although he did not say so in *Up From Slavery*, he said in a later book that he had not gotten enough to eat. Slave ration was a monotonous and skimpy diet of cornbread and salt pork—with two tablespoons of molasses every Sunday. Little Booker used to try to stretch it out by tilting the tin plate so that the molasses would spread and seem more. Anything else he got was stolen. Living in the plantation kitchen had one advantage—the sweet potatoes were kept there in a large hole covered with boards in the middle of the cabin floor. When it was opened, Booker had a chance to filch one. One of his nighttime memories was of his mother waking her children to eat some eggs or a chicken she had cooked for them in the secret hours. Reporting this, Washington made a distinction between the morality of slavery and that of freedom, when nobody was more strict about honesty than his mother: "Taking place at the time it did, and for the reason it did no one could ever make me believe that my mother was guilty of thieving."

If food was scarce, clothing was even more so. Up to the time he was nearly six, Booker wore nothing. He and his brother and baby sister all crawled or toddled about the yard among the numerous outbuildings—the other slave cabins, the springhouse, smokehouse, corncrib, and barn—as naked as the farm animals.

Sometimes other children, both black and white, came to the place, but when John and Booker were big enough for real play—to try fishing in the stream, for instance—they were big enough to be switched for it. They were set to work carrying water to the men in the fields and cleaning up the yard around the house.

Not that the yard ever got a great deal of attention. Weeds grew in it, fences were broken down, gates hung half off their hinges. It was slave work to tend to these things, and on small marginal farms like the Burroughs', no one paid much attention to such details. But the sun gleamed on the leaves of the water oaks, and the mourning dove sounded above the shrilling of the locusts; nature, even as it crowded in on the plantation, was beautiful in itself. It was in these earliest years that Booker learned to "love the soil, to love cows and pigs and trees and flowers and birds and worms and creeping things."

When he was big enough to work outside the confines of the yard, Booker was given his first slave clothing. It consisted of a single shirt, made of a material called tow, which was worn all year round; for cold weather there was a pair of wooden-soled brogans. Booker was proud of the shoes, but the shirt was a misery. It was made of flax spun by Aunt Sophie, who lived in "the weave." The coarsest part of the flax—actually the refuse—was set aside for the slaves. New material from it was like a medieval hair shirt. To Booker's tender skin it felt like dozens of chestnut burrs. It was that or go naked, and he would have flatly chosen the second if he had been allowed to. But John took over

his little brother's shirts at their prickliest and wore them the first few weeks to break them in. John was not only protective and generous; he was tougher and more assertive than his shy little brother. He would have been handsome if it had not been for a cast in one eye, and he was remembered more clearly than Booker by the Burroughs grandchildren as "lively and bright as a dollar."

But John could not shield his brother from everything. The year when the shirt became obligatory was also the year of two dramatic events that hastened growing up in a hard world. In April of 1861, when Booker was five, the war began, and in July his master died. The beginning of the four fighting years was exciting: to the whites because it was adventurous and because they could not conceive of losing, to the Negroes because they hoped that if their masters did lose they would be free. The whole neighborhood was present at the first muster of the Franklin Rangers, the proud Company D of the Second Regiment of Virginia Cavalry. Young Frank and Billie Burroughs were in that group which gathered with its horses—most men had two—in the field at Taylor's Store. Frank and Billie were the only two of the six Burroughs boys to die in the war.

Their father died first, of "lung fever," and was buried on the plantation, beside the road leading down to the house. To a little slave boy this was a much more serious event than the beginning of the war. It was part of a good owner's articles of faith that slaves should not be sold and families broken up except in cases of absolute necessity; but the death of a master was always a time for financial stocktaking. The Burroughs slaves were at once the most valuable and the most negotiable part of the estate. Altogether they were worth $5,500

Hampton's baseball club was later duplicated at Tuskegee.

out of the property's total value of about $10,000.

The will was not probated until November, and during that summer Booker certainly learned that there was a chance he could be sold away from his mother. His master's will provided that he was now the property of his mistress, Elizabeth Robertson Burroughs. But if she should die—or marry again—the property should be divided among the fourteen Burroughs children. All the Burroughs slaves knew about the neighborhood bogeyman, "Tradin' Tom" Dudley, who lived only a few miles away in a big house with an auction block right in his front yard. And they knew of the master's son Tom Burroughs, who also traded in slaves. The rumor was that he had a pot of gold buried down in Georgia; Booker heard the slaves singing a song in the Quarters:

> Mother, is Massa going' to sell, sell us tomorrow?
> Yes, my child! Yes, my child! Yes, my child!
> Goin' to sell us way down in Georgia?
> Yes, yes, yes.

But Elizabeth Burroughs was not going to die—or marry again. She stayed on, and she needed all the slaves to keep the place running. Her five eldest children had married and left home years before, Frank and Billie were off with the Rangers, and only sixteen-year-old Newton was at home with his six sisters. The three elder Burroughs girls were above the old-maid line of twenty-five. And young Eliza, Laura, and little Ellen America were, according to a candid relative, not very pretty, "but better people never lived."

In *Up From Slavery*, Washington makes very few judgments about his owners. The only member of his master's family whom he mentions in the brief, generally nameless account of his owners was young Master Billie, who, before his enlistment, often interceded to save the slaves from being whipped. But Washington corresponded with Laura in later years and asked her down to Tuskegee to see his school. Miss Laura herself had taught school near Halesford, and one of little Booker's chores had been to ride bareback behind her to the schoolhouse, hold the horse while she dismounted, and then take the horse back to the farm, where it was needed for work during the day. At no time did he himself enter the schoolhouse. When he looked in and saw the white children studying the books that were denied to him, he felt that to walk in that door would be "the same as getting into paradise."

As he grew older he took other trips behind Laura's sisters, and the plantation, which had seemed "about as near to nowhere as any locality gets to be," became fixed between certain points. He found out that when you turned right at the gate, the post office of Halesford was about two miles down the pike near the Staunton River. Over the river in Bedford County was the big tobacco market town of Lynchburg. When you turned left toward the post office of Taylor's Store, three miles along, you could go right on to Rocky Mount, the county seat. From there a stagecoach ran over the mountain to Big Lick (later the city of Roanoke). But Booker could go to none of these places without one of his mistresses or a pass from his owners.

There was a group of neighborhood men called the Patrol—in the Quarters they were known as "paterollers"—night riders who looked for slaves absent from their plantations without passes. The patrollers also searched the neighborhood Quarters for arms, and broke up any gathering of Negroes.

One night every week Booker found himself away from the plantation, alone and frightened. The war had brought heavier tasks to the few at home, and one of these was almost more than Washington could manage. He took corn to be ground at Teel's mill, on Indian Run, about three miles from the plantation. The heavy sack of corn on the horse's back was evenly divided on each side when he started out, but when he got on the back-country road that led off the pike there were gullies in the red clay, and steep grades. Inevitably the corn shifted and the sack fell off, carrying the small rider with it as he tried to hold it back. The only thing to do then was to wait for someone to come along who could help lift the sack. On the lonely road this could be hours. It was often after dark when the corn was ground, and the ride back was full of terror. Rustles in the trees could be wolves or wildcats or even army deserters, who were said to cut off the ears of little colored boys. And lateness meant being whipped.

At home his easiest job was in the Big House dining room, where he kept flies off the table at meals by working a large set of paper fans, operated by a pulley. It was here that he picked up most of his knowledge about the white world. As the paper whispered and slapped together and the voices of the family rose above the clatter of crockery, Booker absorbed conversation with a curiosity and retentiveness that they could not have guessed.

They talked mostly about the war, for their involvement was complete. All six of the sons had enlisted, and the household was constantly stirring with news of them; their goings and comings on furlough or sick leave, their wounds—and their deaths. From the time the war began the Burroughs slaves, for all their secret wish that their master's enemies would win the war, could not help sharing in the family's griefs. When young Master Billie died in the spring of 1863 there was sorrow in the Quarters that Booker remembered as "only second to that in the 'Big House' . . . it was no sham sorrow, but real." Frank's death was particularly poignant because he had re-enlisted after being given a medical discharge by the Surgeon General. He died aboard a hospital ship on his way home.

In *Up From Slavery* Washington made a specific point of the fact that the slaves were just as eager to help take care of their wounded young masters as the white relatives. Nursing young Newton must have given everybody one of the war's few light moments. His record soberly stated that he had been wounded "in the right thigh." The family language was simpler: "Uncle Newt got shot in the rump, and he was teased a lot for it. People said he must have been running away and he said, 'well, if you had bullets whizzing all around you, you'd run too.'"

When Newton had left, it meant that there were, for the first time, no white males regularly on the plantation. Washington said in his book what he frequently stressed later in speeches to white southerners: that the behavior of the vast majority of slaves during the war had proved that the Negro should be considered worthy of "a specific trust. . . . The slave who was selected to sleep in the 'big house' during the absence of the males was considered to have the place of honor. Anyone attempting to harm 'young mistress' or 'old mistress' during the night would have had to cross the dead body of the slave to do so."

But with all their personal loyalty, the slaves kept listening for news of northern victories, and in *Up From Slavery* Washington reported that they knew the outcome of every battle. There were a good many poetic ideas about the Negro grapevine—that in some way this child of nature was able to pluck happenings out of the air in an extrasensory manner denied the white man. As Stephen Vincent Benét says in *John Brown's Body*:

> The wind from the brier patch brought him news
> That never went walking in white men's shoes.

Washington gave a simpler explanation: that the slave who went for the mail hung around and listened to the talk at the post office, then told the latest news to other slaves whom he met on the road. He did not mention that on the Burroughs plantation he was sometimes the slave who went for the mail. Nor did he disclose that in the Halesford neighborhood there was another explanation for the mysterious slave grapevine.

Only a mile from Taylor's Store lived a planter called Ol' Menas, who owned twenty-nine slaves. One of them could read. The girl who cleaned the master's room in the morning would sneak out the latest newspaper and return it after it had been read. It would be carefully folded or crumpled as it had been before— but the news in it was already on its way.

In the early months of 1865 every day brought "its news and mutterings of great events." The deserters came out of the woods and walked the main road openly along with whole regiments of discharged soldiers. In the Quarters the singing was louder:

> We'll soon be free,
> When de Lord will call us home.

The momentous news was brought by a stranger who rode down the lane one summer morning. All the slaves were told to gather around the little front porch of the Burroughs home. Booker, Amanda, and John stood close to their mother. Members of the Burroughs family were ranged on either side to listen as the stranger read from a paper what Booker Washington remembered as the President's own Proclamation: that they were then, thenceforward, and forever free. When he had finished reading, the stranger turned to the Negroes and translated in simple terms. They could go now, when and where they pleased. Booker's mother, with tears running down her face, leaned down and kissed him and explained the incredible again—that "this was the day for which she had been so long praying, but fearing that she would never live to see."

That Promised Land which presumably lay all about Jane Ferguson and her family, and nine million other freed slaves, was full of cruel disappointment—and of hope. The long, patient job of making ex-slaves into citizens in fact was the one her son Booker undertook to begin. He did not think that progress would be swift, although he did all he could to hasten it. He knew it would go on after his own lifetime. Before Booker Washington died in 1915, the perceptive journalist Ray Stannard Baker, who knew only part of Washington's work for his race, said of him: "Measured by any standard, white or black, Washington must be regarded today as one of the great men of his country; and in the future he will be so honored." The simple truth is that he has not been honored as he should have been, because his whole story has never been fully known. In the emotional climate of America's most grievous social upheaval, it is time for everyone concerned to consider him again.

The biography of Booker T. Washington from which this article is adapted was begun sixteen years ago by Marquis James. Mr. James, who had twice won the Pulitzer prize for history, felt that a full-scale biography of this complicated man, based on Washington's own papers, local records, and interviews, was long overdue. Mr. James died in 1955 before the research was completed, and his widow undertook to finish the book. This fascinating study will be published by the Houghton Mifflin Company.

Pershing's Island War

CONTINUED FROM PAGE 35

Despite all these precautions, Moros got through. One night in August, a charge overwhelmed one outpost, leaving two men dead and two others slashed and bleeding. Pershing the psychologist decided to become Pershing the warrior. "It's stupid to sit here and let these people shoot us up," he said.

The Captain fired off a message to headquarters at Malabang, on the coast, asking permission to go into action. "Further forbearance might lead friendly Moros also to misjudge our tolerance and take up arms," he warned. He got the go-ahead, and within two weeks he rode out of Camp Vicars at the head of a formidable column. Besides his well-armed, blue-shirted infantry in their broad-brimmed campaign hats, a train of mules carried mountain howitzers and Gatling guns that gave the Americans vastly superior firepower.

Pershing's objective was the *cota* of the sultan of Maciu, a fortress on a promontory on Lake Lanao. It was all but surrounded by water and a formidable swamp. Pershing made a thorough reconnaissance and then ordered his engineers to bridge the swamp.

Sweating and cursing, the Americans went to work. Huge trees came crashing down to be trimmed and pounded into the mucky earth. For two weeks the men labored, while the Moros harassed them by night. Yet the job was finally done, and Pershing swiftly pushed his skirmish lines to within a few hundred feet of the fort. His problems were far from solved. The ancient stronghold loomed above the weary Americans in the shimmering heat, its walls ten feet thick and its wide moat further discouraging a frontal assault. With the Americans in sight, the six hundred Moros inside were creating a horrendous racket by beating their war drums, pounding their gongs, and howling curses and insults—their way of whipping up courage. They were also banging away with ancient cannons and rifles. Over all flew the sultan's long red battle flags.

Pershing called for his artillery. For the time being he was content to let his howitzers drop shell after shell inside the fort.

Toward midnight the crashing, clanging racket within the stronghold reached a kind of climax. The Americans grasped their rifles and checked their bayonets. Then there came a wild cry from the fort: *La ilaha il-la'l-lahu* ("There is no god but Allah"). Out swarmed the Moros, shrieking war cries, while the priests whanged gongs and exhorted them from the walls of the fort.

Pershing's men were ready. The howitzers belched clouds of death-dealing canister. The infantrymen, firing by the volley, coolly blasted the attackers off their feet. Not a Moro reached the American lines.

For the rest of the night the Moro fort was shrouded in silence. When dawn filtered through the thick jungle at their backs, Pershing's men shouted with surprise and delight. The red battle flags were gone. The Moros had decamped by water. In the torn and ripped grass before them the Americans counted twenty bodies, proof that the enemy had retreated in disarray. Traditionally the Moros were careful to retrieve their dead.

But Pershing knew better than to let anyone into the fort. As dawn brightened into day, he insisted on maintaining his lines intact. Within minutes the men saw why. Out of the ditch sprang a half dozen white-robed juramentados, their eyebrows shaved and their hair cut short. Whirling their krises above their heads, they flung themselves at the American lines, only to be met point-blank by volleys that no amount of fanaticism could survive. They toppled in their tracks, and Pershing pronounced the fort of Maciu safe to enter.

After burning as much of it as would take fire, Pershing marched his men through numerous villages along the southern shore of Lake Lanao, where he made it clear that he and not the sultan was now the man in charge. But he reiterated to all the minor datus the assurances he had given to his visitors at Camp Vicars. The Americans wanted only one thing: to see an end to cattle stealing, slave trading, and piracy. To substantiate his word, Pershing kept his men under perfect discipline. Not a Moro woman was touched, nothing was so much as "borrowed" from a native hut.

Elsewhere in the islands the war was not going as well. On Samar, a sixty-man native constabulary unit and its American commanding officer were wiped out in an ambush. Back home the anti-imperialists wrote a letter to President Roosevelt demanding the immediate withdrawal of American forces from the Philippines. When Secretary of War Elihu Root issued a report on the war, he was savagely attacked as a liar and a criminal. The anti-imperialists continued to hold protest meetings around the nation and distributed printed matter attacking government policy.

Meanwhile at Camp Vicars Pershing had another opportunity to show his good intentions. A cholera epidemic broke out in the district, and the Americans were quick to respond with medicine and medical advice. The policy paid off handsomely in good will.

At about the same time Pershing received a visit from the sultan of Bayan, a powerful local war lord, who came to talk peace. Surrounded by attendants, the sultan strutted into Vicars in his fanciest purple vest and red pants. Pershing treated him like a king. He played music for him on a phonograph, gave him an honor guard, feasted him royally, and all but drowned him in effusive flattery. The sultan responded by swearing eternal friendship and fidelity to the Americans.

"Your Honor," said Pershing when the sultan was about to leave, "I'm going to return your compliment by visiting you." The sultan looked dismayed, but was too proud to tell Pershing that he did not care to have American soldiers on his doorstep.

A month later, then, a heavily escorted Pershing appeared before the sultan's imposing fort, high on a mountainside. Up the ladders, which were the only access to the place, climbed Pershing and his men—who then raised the American flag. Coolly eyeing the sultan and his swarm of followers, with the inevitable carving knives on their hips, Pershing said: "Your Honor will, I hope, permit us to fire a salute to our flag."

Once more the sultan could only agree, and at a nod from Pershing the gunners cut loose with twenty-one blasts. They fired live ammunition into the jungle, and the Moros were properly impressed. This was Pershing's way of making sure that the sultan's retainers would be "courteous and friendly." The sultan now became so enthusiastic about Pershing that he pronounced himself prepared to consecrate the Christian American chief a datu. This was truly an unprecedented honor and Pershing accepted it with utter seriousness; he knew that it would give him tremendous influence with Moros everywhere.

Back at Vicars, Pershing was soon so highly regarded by many Moros that he could write to a friend: "If I should say: 'Go and kill this man or that,' the next day they would appear in camp with his head." He did not, of course, pursue such tactics; he continued to preach peace and prosperity. But only the Moros in the vicinity of Camp Vicars were inclined to listen. The sultan of Bacolod, commanding some six hundred warriors and a series of forts high on the western shore, remained a rambunctious rebel. He regularly sent nasty letters to Camp Vicars, insisting that the Americans convert to Mohammedanism, stop eating pork, and march in a body to Bacolod, where his chief priest "will practice circumcision upon you." The sultan had truculent allies on those three sides of the big lake where the American presence was not immediate.

Early in 1903, Pershing decided to take a gamble. He would march his command all the way around the lake, punishing the rebel bands one by one. His first target was the sultan of Bacolod and his warriors. They greeted the Americans with the usual clangor of gongs and unfurling of battle flags. The sultan contemptuously ignored Pershing's demand for an immediate surrender. He thought he could afford to be arrogant. His fort was considered impregnable. Like the stronghold of Maciu, it was on the lake shore, with a moat forty feet deep and thirty-five feet wide; its earthen and bamboo walls were twenty feet thick. The bamboo-reinforced mud roof was practically bomb-proof. Just behind the parapet, there was a covered subway that ran all the way around the fort. And these Moros had modern weapons: Mauser and Remington bullets sang past the head of any American who showed himself. This time Pershing could not afford a siege. He had to strike hard and fast before other sultans in the neighborhood caught war fever and started hacking away at his rear.

For two days, Pershing softened up the fort with artillery. Firing from ridges above the lake, the gunners were able to drop shells accurately into the well between the outer parapet and the rest of the fort. But they did little or no damage to the roof except to demolish the huge war flags—which sent the Moros into frenzies of rage.

Then suddenly, without warning, the Americans found themselves facing another formidable enemy. Behind the lines, one, two, three, a half dozen men were prostrate in their tents, retching and fouling their bedding. It was cholera. Pershing enforced the most stringent sanitary procedures; all water had to be boiled, no food whatsoever was to be bought from a native. But more men sickened, and two died on successive days. Now an assault became an absolute necessity: with cholera at their backs, the men's morale would disintegrate in a long siege.

On the afternoon of the third day, the Americans moved forward behind a curtain of cannon and machine-gun fire. Suddenly there was a cry of anguish from the first skirmish line. The long grass was thick with pointed bamboo stakes. Then came a crash (and a string of profanity): someone had fallen into a camouflaged pit. Bleeding, bruised, and fighting mad, the Americans finally reached the edge of the moat. The Moros blazed away through the crenels in the parapet, but their aim was atrocious.

Behind the assault companies came detachments lugging several huge trees, which they toppled across the ditch, creating shaky, makeshift bridges. The engineers threw brush and branches into the ditch under them for those who lost their balance. Two sergeants, a corporal, and a lieutenant tightroped across, followed by a company of the 27th Infantry. At least a half dozen men wound up flat on their backs on the brush below. But, said Arnold Henry Savage Landor, an English reporter on the scene, they "climbed like cats up the steep wall" and joined in the wild brawl that was developing on the parapet.

Moros came rushing to meet the Americans, swinging *campilans*—huge, two-handed swords. Sergeant Samuel Hafer, the third man up on the wall, had his arm lopped off. The huge parapet was like a small mountain, and the Moros had burrowed all sorts of secret passageways through it. A private named Cosser was attacked from behind by two natives who sprang out of one of these holes. He knocked one into the ditch with the butt of his rifle and shot the other, but in ten flashing seconds Cosser was bleeding in six places. As the regimental surgeon bent over the bleeding Hafer, the chief priest of Bacolod leaped from another secret tunnel, waving a campilan. The doctor clouted him in the chest with his fist, and sent him spinning into the ditch. According to Landor, he was shot full of holes before he hit the bottom. Meanwhile, up and down the parapet Americans were proving that a bayonet in the hands of a well-trained soldier was more than equal to a Moro's kris. In five minutes there was not a living Moro left on the parapet.

The troops swarmed forward, over the subway and up onto the roof of the fort. The Moros inside were howling war cries. To clean them out man by man would have cost Pershing dozens of casualties. Instead, he ordered brush shoved through an opening in the roof; kerosene was applied, and it was ignited. In five minutes the fort was an inferno. Pershing pulled back his men and sat on the safe side of the ditch until a tremendous explosion blew the roof off Bacolod.

A quick body count taken in the still-burning fort showed thirty Moro soldiers dead on the top floor. Pershing had smashed the strongest fort on Mindanao in a frontal assault that cost him just three men wounded and none killed.

If Pershing was pleased by the results of the battle, others were not. The hostile Manila *American* headlined: "BACOLOD MOROS SLAUGHTERED WITH KRAGS." But Pershing and his fellow officers were under orders to make no reply to such criticism. He simply pushed his weary men forward, determined to complete his march around the lake. At another trouble spot, Calahui, he earned a dividend from his swift reduction of Bacolod. Instead of slugging it out, the Calahui fort surrendered after a brief bombardment, and the Calahui sultans and datus met the Americans with smiles and escorts.

But soon Pershing was in territory where no white soldier had ever marched before. Three more times he had to send his infantrymen over the walls of defiant forts. As at Bacolod, each attack was meticulously planned and flawlessly executed. Although there were times when the engineers had to corduroy a road through swamps, and mules and horses had to be all but carried through jungle mud, Pershing completed his circuit of the lake in six weeks. By then the entire region had sullenly conceded that the American datu was a fighting man more than equal to the toughest son of Allah. Back home, news of the whirlwind campaign, which cost less than twenty American lives (some were cholera victims), thrilled the entire country. Landor said that Uncle Sam owed the pacification of the Lake Lanao region "entirely to the tact, consideration and patience and strategic skill" of Captain John J. Pershing. And then the writer added: "If there is one man who deserves to be made a Brigadier General, it is this gallant officer."

Pershing was by now showing symptoms of battle fatigue. He had been in the Philippines for almost thirty-six months, eighteen of them in the nerve-stretching tension of Camp Vicars. The doctors, against Pershing's protests, sent him home. Theodore Roosevelt, in his annual address to Congress, singled him out as an answer to the anti-imperialists' attempt to picture American soldiers as brainless butchers. He added: "When a man renders such service as Captain Pershing . . . it ought to be possible to reward him." But the Army system of promotion by seniority, which Congress refused to change, left the President helpless.

As for the anti-imperialists, there was a strange note of defeat in the oratory at their 1903 meeting. Harvard's great psychologist, William James, warned: "To the ordinary citizen, anti-imperialism is something petrified, a religion that means only to prophesy and denounce." He advised them to stop protesting the war and work on a plan for Philippine independence.

The guerrilla war slowly flickered out, but not without further incident. At Zamboanga on Mindanao, Moros charged into the very heart of Army headquarters and killed the commanding general's secretary. On one northern island, members of a native constabulary company rebelled, assassinated their American commander, and had to be hunted down.

Captain Pershing, meanwhile, was still on Roosevelt's mind. Fuming over his defeat by the Army lobby on the promotion issue, he sent Pershing to the Army

War College, kept him on duty in Washington as a military attaché for a year, and then decided to jump him—over the heads of 862 senior officers—directly to brigadier general. Although the President cannot promote officers to lower ranks, the right to appoint generals belongs exclusively to him.

Late in 1906 Pershing returned to the Philippines, where eventually he was made the military governor of Moro Province. He played a key role in the drawn-out process of final pacification. In 1913 he led his men in a last pitched battle, which crushed some five hundred rebellious Moros holed up in Mount Bagsak, an extinct volcano on the island of Jolo. When one of his captains was killed in the assault, Pershing himself joined the kris-swinging, bayonet-slashing melee with highly ungeneral-like enthusiasm.

The news of the fight brought a last flicker of protest from the anti-imperialists at home. But Pershing stood his ground and replied that the rebels were "notorious cattle thieves and murderers." William Cameron Forbes, the U.S. governor general of the Philippines, backed him wholeheartedly, declaring that Pershing had "exercised the utmost patience in endeavoring to appeal to the reason of the Moro people and in avoiding a recourse to arms."

Six months later Pershing sailed for home. Soon, after a frustrating chase after another guerrilla leader, Pancho Villa, in Mexico, "Black Jack" would be making history on a larger scale—as commander in chief of American doughboys in World War I. As for the now pacified Moros, they paid him the kind of tribute Pershing probably understood better than any other American: they promoted him from datu to sultan.

Mr. Fleming, the author of our Verdicts of History series, is one of the magazine's most frequent contributors. Among the sources for the current article was Richard O'Connor's Black Jack Pershing *(Doubleday, 1961).*

A Warm Evening at the Rock

CONTINUED FROM PAGE 39

and then over that hodgepodge of hemp, spare fire hose, and the two glass demijohns of turpentine. Reaching over a shelf of miscellaneous tools and spare parts, Sutton got hold of the beam scale, but in doing so he knocked over a heavy iron wrench, which fell onto one of the demijohns and smashed it into a thousand pieces. The turpentine poured out into the hemp and trickled down through the loose floor boards. Damn, what a mess, thought Sutton. He took the beam scale up on deck and started back to wipe up the spilled turpentine. He got as far as the forward ladder. . . .

Clum was still holding the light for Allen when he noticed the little stream of liquid coming down through the floor boards immediately over his head. Must be, he thought, that Sutton had knocked over one of the buckets of water Clum had seen earlier in the storeroom—Damn, right into the felt we've spent all this time on. . . . "Why are you spilling water on us?" Clum shouted up to Sutton. Then Clum smelled it and knew it wasn't water. He did not report this interesting little happening because there was no officer on hand to report it to. They worked on for six or seven minutes longer, until the twine broke and the whole sorry mess of turpentine-soaked felt fell down right into the open light that was sitting on the valve-stem guide.

At five minutes past eight the Irish boatswain's mate, whom the crew called "the Member from Clare" on account of his below-decks politicking, was comfortably seated on the hammock nettings directing the coal loading when he saw smoke coming out of the forward hatch. He yelled, "Ring the bell! Ring the bell! Fire! Fire!" and without further ado jumped directly over the side right into one of the coal barges. Someone did ring the bell. And the drummer boy produced at least one roll on his drum before he dropped it, ran aft, and jumped through the stern port into the water.

"Oh, Jesus, the ship is on fire," yelled a marine, and he too took to the water.

The Spanish coal-bargemen, their nerves frayed by the precipitate arrival of the Member from Clare in their midst, cried out, *"Fuego, fuego!" "El buque está encendido, perderemos el bote, larga!" "Corta!" "Corta!"* Their voices rose in a hysterical crescendo. Cutting their barge loose, they rowed for their lives.

The *Missouri* ran up emergency blue lights that the Rock answered by firing a signal gun. H.M.S. *Malabar* fired her forty-two-pounder. Nearly enough guns for the day, one might think, what with the governor's salute, Prince Albert's birthday, and morning and evening gunfire at the dockyard; but not quite enough—not yet. There would be two more. The crew of Captain

Newton's gig manned their boat and awaited orders. Someone even remembered to post a sentry over the liquor locker.

Lieutenant Bissell, senior officer on board, had been enjoying his ease in the officers' wardroom. The O.D.'s messenger was just reporting "All galley fires and eight o'clock lights out" when Bissell, hearing the commotion, rushed up on the spar deck to see what was going on. The bell was ringing, the drum was drumming, and all hell was breaking loose. Bissell immediately saw that he might have to cope with not one but two eventualities: the ship burning up, or worse—if the fire reached the powder magazines—blowing up.

Trying to locate the source of the fire, Bissell ran forward along the spar deck, then down the hatch to the passage between the galley and the engine room, thence back to the open deck, and to the forward hatch where smoke was coming up. Here he found the forecastle sailors, who had assembled the unwieldy force pump, run out the hose, and were screwing on the nozzle—but so slowly that Bissell grabbed the nozzle and screwed it on himself.

Next Bissell turned his attention to the two powder magazines, one at each end of the ship, both full of black powder, the most explosive substance known. The keys for the magazines were in the Captain's cabin at the other end of the ship. Bissell ran and got them, and ordered the gunner to unlock the forward magazine, which was closest to the fire, and flood it with water. With that peril over, the gunner was to go aft, unlock the other magazine, and await orders.

Meanwhile, Bissell went down to the engine room. There he saw Lieutenant Faron and his men dousing the fire with buckets of water that were being passed to the scene from amidships.

By this time the gunner had been gone five minutes, which seemed an eternity to Bissell, and still there was no report that he had been able to flood the forward magazine. When he did show up shortly, he brought the bad news that he had not been able to get there through all the smoke and fire. Bissell grabbed the keys from him and went to flood the magazine himself. On the berth deck a solid wall of smoke stopped him short and the fierce heat drove him back. He tried another route, lowering himself through a small hatch near the bowsprit, but quickly found that no man could survive there a minute. There seemed no hope. For the first time the enormity of actually losing everything confronted him—for most assuredly the fire would soon reach the magazine and blow the ship to kingdom come.

With this overwhelming thought in mind, Bissell went back to the engine room to consult with Lieutenant Faron. Was there any chance at all of putting the fire out? Faron replied, "I don't know. I think it doubtful." Bissell had to resolve that doubt. He considered that the most extreme measures were justified. "Open up the Kingston valves," Bissell ordered with finality, "take off the handhole plates of the condensers." Sea water would then rush into the boilers, thence into the condensers, and out through the open handholes into the ship. The ship would of course be flooded and would probably sink, but the black powder would be rendered innocuous and a fearful explosion precluded —or so Bissell hoped.

Seeing that there was no further need for him in the engine room, Bissell returned to the open spar deck—to more bad news. Lieutenant Hunter, in charge amidships, was standing on top of the paddle-wheel housing in order to better direct the bucket brigade; he asked Bissell if he didn't think it would be a good idea to send the gig into the landing to pick up the Captain. With this shattering remark Bissell realized, twenty minutes after the fire started, that he had committed the cardinal sin of not informing the Captain of impending disaster.

At this moment Captain Newton was making his way along the streets of Gibraltar toward the waterfront, through excited crowds shouting, "*El vapor del frigate Americano es del fuego!*" The whole bay was in an uproar while Newton cooled his heels waiting for the boat that his second-in-command had forgotten to send in. It was no wonder that Rodman Price thought him "highly excited." At long last he found himself in his gig. While six expert oarsmen strained to get him back, his once-beautiful ship was burning up before his very eyes. Finally the gig pulled alongside, the quartermaster was hailing, in age-old custom, "Boat ahoy!" and the gig's coxswain was replying, "*Missouri,*" meaning that the Captain was returning. It was 9:00 P.M. The ship had been on fire for an hour.

Newton climbed up to the top of the starboard paddle-wheel housing, and from this vantage point took hold of the situation with long-accustomed assurance. His first command, "Silence!" brought some semblance of order out of the chaos of noise and confusion. Next, he ordered all the hatches closed in an effort to contain the fire. Then he sent fresh men to relieve the weary pumpers forward. All around him buckets passed in rapid succession, but he could not fail to notice that no water was coming from the aft force pump, and that the hose from the forward pump was too short. There were no other pumps, and the new India-rubber hoses he had brought from Washington had no couplings on them. There was not much else he could do.

Around him the harbor was alive with boats either rushing to the rescue or simply moving to get a better view of the fire. At the Waterport Gate the Governor himself sent off a relief expedition from the Royal Irish Sappers. Sir George Sartorious personally led them out to the ship. A British officer brought out thirty-six convicts from the dockyard as volunteer firemen. Captain Graham, from the American bark *Pons*, came over to help the sailing master save his navigational equipment. Cushing rushed out in time to save his diplomatic papers and the letter from President Tyler to the Emperor, but he could not save his gorgeous uniform for the Dragon Throne audience. The *Malabar*'s pinnace, carrying men equipped with portable fire pumps, axes, and fire buckets, pulled up directly under the *Missouri*'s fore chains and pumped a steady stream of water into the hull. At ten minutes to ten the *Locust* came within fifty yards of the *Missouri* to tow her out farther. It was too late. The frigate, filled with sea water from pump and bucket, valve and boat, was already resting on the bottom in that shallow spot the *Locust*'s crew had viewed with disapproval yesterday evening.

By ten o'clock the flames had nearly penetrated to the sixty tons of coal that had been loading all day. Lieutenant Faron and his gang of engineers had to abandon the engine room. Unable to stand any longer on the hot decks of the forecastle, they had to abandon that too, together with the forecastle force pump. Only buckets and the portable pumps of the relief expeditions now stood between the *Missouri* and ultimate disaster, and considering the immensity of the fire, these puny efforts seemed, said a man in the *Locust*, like "spitting on it."

It was as light as midday in the harbor. Never had there been such a sight at Gibraltar since the day in 1704 when Admiral Sir George Rooke wrested the Rock from Spain with red-hot shot. From her station at the maintop, Bess could see the sheets of flame spreading from the hatches to the hammock nettings, licking up through the rigging toward her. She started down to the deck.

The *Missouri* was *in extremis*.

It was now eleven o'clock. Captain Newton, only short hours ago at the pinnacle of his career, in command of the greatest, newest warship in the U.S. Navy, entrusted with the safe passage of an important minister of state, now stood on another kind of pinnacle, the high housing of the starboard paddle wheel, in stark relief against the flaming wreckage. The flames would soon engulf that pinnacle—but first there was an inevitable decision, a final order only he could give. He called a final officers' conference up there on the paddle-wheel housing. They had to move fast, for the decks were about to cave in. The decision was made. Newton gave his last order: "Save yourselves!"

Men jumped overboard from all manner of places— through portholes, off the rigging, from yards and masts—before the fascinated eyes of watchers along the yardarms of the *Malabar*, on the deck of the *Locust*, and in the scores of boats of the sightseeing flotilla. Seven *Missouri* crewmen crawled along the lower studding-sail boom waiting their chance, and were thrown bodily into the water when the topping lift parted. Hitherto reluctant for fear of explosions, boats closed in from every direction to pick up survivors, many of whom were very poor swimmers.

At 11:15 the Captain climbed down the Jacob's ladder to his gig, which this time was waiting for him. In the tradition of the sea he was the last to leave the ship. But no . . . there was a movement aft, on the tip of the spanker boom where it jutted out over the stern. A boat moved in to the rescue. Arms reached up. It was the bear. The upstretched arms scared her. She fought back like a drowning person, broke away, waddled along the burning decks in a last desperate effort to regain her station on the maintop. Then Bess, the *Missouri*'s amulet against accident, was swallowed up by the flames and roasted alive.

A broken skeleton on the harbor floor was all that was left of the once-proud Missouri. *She had sunk in such shallow water that she was a hazard to navigation, and the wreckage had to be painstakingly removed by divers piece by piece.*

While Captain Newton approached the bottom rung of the dangling Jacob's ladder he could think, during this last split second, that the *Missouri* was still a commissioned unit of the Navy; but the moment his fingers let go that last rung and he dropped into his gig, that moment she became a wreck, a menace to navigation, a nuisance to the authorities, a costly salvage problem for the United States, a mere port captain's notice to mariners that "great precautions must be taken by the masters of vessels entering at night . . ." He dropped into the gig and was rowed away.

But Newton could neither shut his eyes to what was happening nor stop his ears to it. The forecastle deck fell in, carrying with it the two ten-inch guns, which exploded one after the other, as if in final salute to the disastrous day. Flames leapt to the top of the mainmast. The main-topsail yard plummeted into the web of rigging. Seven minutes after Newton let go that last rung, the whole tremendous mainmast with all its yards and topmasts fell to the deck with a sickening crash. At twenty-eight minutes before midnight the foremast also came crashing down, followed by the

mizzenmast. Only the smokestack, gaunt and glowing red, remained standing. At midnight it too dropped into a grave formed by the iron skeletons of the burnt-out paddle wheels.

At 3:20 A.M. the forward powder magazine, which had never been flooded, finally blew up, shattering the whole forefront of the hull. The force of the explosion broke windows ashore, even shook men out of their bunks in the *Locust*.

The crew of the steam warship *Missouri,* rescued to the last man, was glad enough to be safe on board the sailing warship *Malabar.* The night of August 26, 1843, was over.

In due course, Captain Newton returned to the United States for his inevitable court-martial, one of those troublesome formalities that captains have to go through on such occasions. The court found that the accused:

Kept on board turpentine in glass vessels immediately over the machinery in a storeroom with loose floor boards.

Allowed the demijohns to be stored with combustible materials in the starboard engineers' storeroom, although he did not order them stored there.

Allowed naked lights to be used in the engine room; but that their use was justified by necessity.

Did not keep the pumps in order.

Did not inspect properly.

Failed to maintain such regulations as the safety of the steamship required.

And finally: "the charge is proved and the court do therefore adjudge Captain John Thomas Newton to be suspended from duty for the term of two years."

On November 21, 1844, President Tyler, who had so gaily waved good-bye to the *Missouri* on her triumphant departure, signed his approval of the court-martial's findings in an uncertain handwriting that seemed to say, "I hate to do this, but it is my duty." As if to prove it, on March 3, 1845, as one of his last executive acts, Tyler remitted Newton's punishment.

The old sea dog returned to duty and again took up the thread of his naval career, now winding to a quiet close. He commanded navy yards first at Pensacola, Florida, and then at Portsmouth, New Hampshire; finally, he commanded the U.S. Home Squadron. At the age of sixty-five, in 1857, while serving as a member of a court of enquiry on someone else for a change, Captain John Thomas Newton died of apoplexy.

Scarritt Adams is a retired captain, U.S. Navy, who spends most of his time in Bermuda but also lectures on American history at the University of Maryland. He specializes in writing about sea disasters. The drawing on page 104 is by Russell Peterson.

second inaugural ball and banquet, an event attended by more than four thousand guests. Women in silks and laces, men in court dress, formal evening attire, or "dazzling uniforms" thronged up the majestic stone stairway into the great south portico, brilliantly illuminated by gas lamps, and ascended the magnificent curving staircase to the grand exhibition hall above. Here, according to newspaper accounts, they admired the columns, the vaulted ceiling and skylight, "elegant tessellated marble floors," and the "Pompeiian style" tiles. In the enormous east hall, with its thirty-two marble pillars, an orchestra played for dancing until 10 P.M., when the military band struck up "Hail to the Chief" and President and Mrs. Lincoln and their entourage strolled into the hall. After midnight there was a monumental feast at 250-foot tables; some guests stayed on until 4:00 A.M.

After the return of peace the building never again achieved such a moment of splendor, but each year thousands of Americans came to see the ever-growing collection of patent models and other curios—including the original of the Declaration of Independence; Benjamin Franklin's printing press; George Washington's field tent, uniform, sword, and commission as Commander in Chief of the Continental Army; and some of Robert E. Lee's personal effects. Then, in late September of 1877, a disastrous fire broke out, and before it could be brought under control, fire engines had arrived from as far away as Baltimore. Many patent models and historical displays were rescued, but the upper portion of the building was so gutted that the interior had to be rebuilt. It is the result of that restoration that one sees today.

In 1932 the Patent Office moved out and the Civil Service Commission took over (and immediately signalled its possession by vandalizing the interior of the building—including the beautiful marble columns—with paint of a color known to every government employee as "civil service green"); two years later the fine flight of steps leading to the south portico was removed to permit the widening of F Street; and in 1953 the structure was more seriously threatened when legislation—backed by local merchants—was introduced in Congress to permit it to be razed and replaced by a parking garage. Happily for the building, for Washington, and for posterity, David E. Finley, the Chairman of the Commission of Fine Arts, called the matter to President Eisenhower's attention and the building was saved; Senator Hubert Humphrey introduced the bill to Congress that spared it.

Then, in 1962, the availability of space in the Old Patent Office Building and the need for a home for the National Portrait Gallery came in conjunction, and made for one of those happy marriages of convenience of which even bureaucracy is sometimes capable. At that, it was something of a shotgun affair. Andrew Mellon, who had presented the National Gallery of Art to the nation in 1937, left a bequest of a number of American portraits to that gallery, with instructions that any not actually needed should go to a national *portrait* gallery, should such a place be in existence twenty years hence. The Mellon trust made the gift in 1942, and precisely twenty years later Congress passed legislation creating the National Portrait Gallery, as a consequence of which thirty-five portraits were transferred to it from the National Gallery of Art.

This stimulus required a response from those charged with administering the will of Congress—the National Portrait Gallery Commission. It suddenly became important that that body do some philosophizing about portraiture in general and about a gallery of national portraits in particular. Among the many considerations were: What was the attitude of the United States government regarding portraits? Which men and women from the American past deserved a place in this pantheon? What criteria should be established to determine the quality of portraits to be hung? Would portraits of living persons be admitted? If so, which living persons? Would the gallery accept a picture of *anyone* from a donor? And finally, and most important, what constitutes a portrait?

In their search for an answer to the last question, it is doubtful that the commissioners' thoughts went back across the centuries to prehistoric times, but that, in truth, is when portraiture began. The art of counterfeiting a likeness of an individual human being had its roots in the desire of primitive peoples to "trap" the spirit of a dead person (usually an ancestor) by making a likeness of him. Sometimes this took the form of a stone carving, like those on Easter Island, sometimes that of a plastered skull decorated to represent a certain individual. But in the sense in which we tend to think of portraiture—that is, the representation of a known personage—the first portrait of an identifiable historic figure is probably one of Narmer, the first pharaoh, who unified Upper and Lower Egypt about 3200 B.C.

The ancient Near East and the Old Kingdom of Egypt set high store by portraiture; the Greeks, on the other hand, were not much concerned with it until Alexander brought back the notion from the East. Not until Roman times did a real portrait tradition begin, reaching its apogee in the wonderfully realistic, psychologically revealing portrait busts of the soldier-emperors, in which the uncompromising honesty of the artist produced minutely observed facial details—portraiture, it might be said, with the warts. For a thousand years Roman political and military leaders were honored for their achievements by having their likenesses put on public display, and posterity is richer for the custom. Then, for nearly another millennium, the tradition lay dormant. The early Christians, with their Judaic suspicion of idolatry and their eyes on another world, were too busy or too uncaring about the world around them to wish to record it.

During the Middle Ages the collecting of sculpture, a custom so highly regarded in earlier times, fell from favor; and instead, the taste of those who could afford such treasures turned more to jewelry, to rich fabrics, and to illuminated manuscripts. With the exception of some death masks of royal personages, portraiture was not really resumed until the fourteenth century, when a few sculptors began to create realistic likenesses of individual subjects. Then, with the Renaissance revival of interest in the classical world and the concept of the dignity of man, portraiture again began to thrive. In painting, it usually took the form of a likeness of the donor discreetly placed in a religious scene; gradually, royalty and the great merchant princes began commissioning separate portraits of themselves.

Along toward the end of the eighteenth century there was a great deal of experimentation going on with the camera obscura; a vogue for silhouette portraits, many of them traced from the shadow of the sitter's profile, had inspired much of it—and as a result of the many efforts made to record these shadows on light-sensitive materials, by the 1840's photography was a practical process. Portraiture, in the form of the photographic likeness, finally came to the masses.

More or less concurrently—by the middle of the nineteenth century, that is—the English had determined that they needed a national portrait gallery. They had always admired portraiture, to such an extent that when there were no British artists capable of recording the likenesses of their great men, talent was imported from the Continent or the great men went abroad to have their portraits painted. But admiration of itself does not build a portrait gallery, and to Philip Henry, fifth Earl Stanhope, goes credit for launching the institution which preserves so many countenances of England's past; in 1856 he proposed in the House of Lords that Queen Victoria consider the possibility of forming "a Gallery of the Portraits of the most eminent Persons in British History." In this effort he was materially aided by the historian Thomas Carlyle, who had written, in a letter to a

friend, the best possible advertisement for such a gallery: ". . . in all my poor Historical investigations," Carlyle said, "it has been . . . one of the most primary wants to procure a bodily likeness of the personage inquired after; a good *Portrait* if such exists; failing that, even an indifferent if sincere one. In short, *any* representation, made by a faithful human creature, of that Face and Figure, which *he* saw with his eyes, and which I can never see with mine, is now valuable to me, and much better than none at all."

In hitting upon certain rules for their own national portrait gallery, the British answered many questions that would confront their American cousins a century

The interior of the Patent Office looked like this in 1856, with patent models and other Americana crowded chockablock.

later. The first requisite was that the celebrity of the subject—not the merit of the artist—would determine whether or not a portrait was to be acquired. In other words, the gallery would be filled on historical, not artistic, grounds. And there would be villains along with heroes: "Nor will [the trustees] consider great faults and errors," the rules read, "even though admitted on all sides, as any sufficient ground for excluding any portrait which may be valuable as illustrating the history of the country." Portraits of living persons, except for the reigning sovereign, were ruled out (similarly, the U.S. National Portrait Gallery plans to include portraits of all Presidents, living or dead); so were modern copies of original portraits (a practice our own gallery cannot wholly avoid).

A nation conscious of its history and its heroes ought to have a sacellum where they are not so much enshrined as they are made available for figurative

109

consultation and quiet inspiration. In this country we like to look our men in the face and see the stuff they are made of, to press the flesh and take their measure. So it is important to us, as it was to the British over a century ago, to possess a national family album. What is then at issue is who shall be included and, practically speaking, how the likenesses of those chosen are to be obtained. Lord Stanhope, serenely contemplating the eight centuries of English history since the Conquest, could say of his proposed portrait gallery: "There ought not to be in this collection a single portrait as to which a man of good education passing round and seeing the name in the catalogue would be under the necessity of asking, 'Who is he?'" Similarly, the act of Congress under which the U.S. gallery was authorized prescribed that the portraits in it should be of men and women who had made "significant contributions" to the history and development and culture of the nation, and in interpreting this, Charles Nagel, the first director of the National Portrait Gallery, stated his belief that the contribution need not be a positive one. In his view, "Aaron Burr would be just as welcome as Alexander Hamilton, or John Wilkes Booth as Abraham Lincoln. For, though the contribution of these men, who were more than common assassins, was far from constructive, no one can doubt that the direction of the country's history was changed by what they did."

But given agreement with Lord Stanhope's criterion for selection, the dilemma for a younger nation—particularly for a nation that began its portrait gallery a century too late—is that most good portraits of even reasonably prominent historical personages are already in other collections. Portraiture, being a costly affair, was not something the average American indulged himself in more than once in a lifetime, and the consequence is that portraits of many notables are relatively unavailable. The gallery would like nothing better, for instance, than to have an important, full-length painting of the country's first President as a keystone of its collection. There are actually two such pictures in private hands and thus potentially available, but one is in the possession of the Earl of Rosebery, who has stated flatly that it is not for sale, and the other is obtainable for $350,000, several times the annual acquisition budget of the National Portrait Gallery. (This portrait, incidentally, is presently on loan to the gallery and is the picture visible at the end of the hall in the photograph on page 4; although the head and

Mr. Ketchum is the managing director of the American Heritage book division, and a member of this magazine's Editorial Committee. He writes the Faces From the Past feature which appears from time to time in our pages.

one hand may have been painted by Gilbert Stuart, a less certain craftsman handled the body and other details and managed to make the Father of his Country look a little like a short turkey with an oversize head.) Certainly a national portrait gallery worth its salt ought to have a likeness of *every* President of the United States, but this, too, is a difficult matter for an institution so newly on the scene. There is, for example, only one known oil painting of Andrew Johnson as President, and it resides in a Swiss museum that is unlikely to part with it. The gallery would give a good deal for that—or for a portrait of John Adams, or Jefferson, or Madison, or Theodore Roosevelt, but in each case likenesses are rare or hard to come by—even for a price.

The acquisition problem, difficult under any circumstances, is made more so by restrictions placed by Congress upon the gallery's permanent collection. The enabling legislation stipulated that the term "portraiture" meant "painted or sculptured likenesses." Which rules out, among other likenesses, those taken with a camera, or a substantial percentage of all likenesses made during the past century and a quarter, when the dominant form of portraiture was photography, not painting. Congress, being part of a bureaucracy, behaves in a manner common to officialdom: it is in the nature of things that each branch of government has its special fields of interest which must be protected at all costs, and in the case of photography, the Library of Congress was adjudged to have prior claim. To put it another way, the will of Congress means that the National Portrait Gallery is to have *no* portrait of President Andrew Johnson if it cannot pry loose the one known painting of him from that Swiss museum; it is not permitted to resort to a fine cabinet photograph of him. A different problem arises in the case of U. S. Grant: the gallery possesses a rather pedestrian oil painting of the general made at the time of Vicksburg, but though the essential Grant is more likely to be found in one of Mathew Brady's or Alexander Gardner's photographs, the gallery cannot include them except in its archival collection.

Unfortunately, the art of portraiture—at least in the sense of official portraits of well-known figures—has been in a state of decline for much of this century. Relatively few illustrious men and women of recent times have sat for their portraits by important artists; it has been easier, less expensive, and occasionally more fashionable to have one's likeness taken by Steichen or Karsh or Bachrach or Newman. To make life more difficult for the portrait painter, the law is on the sitter's side. If a man commissions a portrait and stipulates that the end result must be a likeness acceptable to him, courts have ruled that he cannot be made to pay for one he finds unsatisfactory.

The most prominent dispute of this kind in recent years was the episode involving a portrait of President Lyndon B. Johnson by Peter Hurd. Unfortunately, when the painting was completed the artist shipped it to the L.B.J. Ranch ahead of his own arrival, asking the President not to look at it until Hurd could hang and light it properly. When he arrived at the ranch, Hurd perceived at once that the picture had been uncrated and that the President did not like it. "That's the ugliest thing I ever saw," L.B.J. was quoted as saying. When Hurd asked what type of picture he would prefer, the President showed the artist a painting of himself by illustrator Norman Rockwell. Hurd departed in icy politeness, and the portrait was returned to him. In this case, payment was proffered, but Hurd rejected it. Despite this rhubarb, it seems reasonable to suggest that Hurd's picture will one day be hung in the National Portrait Gallery. It certainly qualifies for admission: it is a portrait of a President done by a distinguished American artist.

It goes almost without saying that the present lot of pictures in the National Portrait Gallery is a very mixed bag. Only the smallest fraction of the total represents the conscious choice of the gallery staff; virtually everything else is a hand-me-down from the National Gallery of Art, or from the Smithsonian Institution, or came in as an unsolicited donation.

This is not to say that there are not good pictures in the collection, or pictures that satisfy the director and his staff: there are some paintings and pieces of sculpture that are superb by any standards—pictures that qualify on grounds of artistic as well as historic worth, as witness the pictures reproduced on pages 8 to 11. And although the collection is as yet much too sparse, it has in it the beginnings of a good representation of the whole spectrum of America's past, from Pocahontas to Dwight David Eisenhower. Looking at the five-hundred-odd portraits that constitute it, one begins to get a sense of what, one day, it might conceivably be, provided that the public and Congress are generous. The National Portrait Gallery, left to its own devices and an acquisition budget of $100,000 annually, is not likely to acquire more than a handful of really good portraits in a day when a fine one sells for as much as $50,000. What it might become will be suggested more dramatically in October of this year, when the gallery opens its doors for the first time and reveals, not its own collection, but a loan exhibition of portraits that have been gathered from public and private sources all over the world—portraits of the character and quality the National Portrait Gallery would like to have. Indeed, if it is to grow and prosper as a truly national gallery, as a pantheon of the nation's great on the site L'Enfant once envisioned for it, such portraits are the kind it richly deserves.

A PAINTER and THREE PRESIDENTS

The reaction of Lyndon Johnson to Peter Hurd's portrait of him is hardly unique in the annals of presidential paintings. But there was one painter—the most celebrated portraitist of his time—who turned the tables and voiced his displeasure with not one but three Presidents.

In 1903, at the invitation of the First Lady, John Singer Sargent went to Washington to paint a portrait of Theodore Roosevelt. From the beginning the two men did not get on. On the very first day, when Sargent roamed through the White House looking for a place to work, Roosevelt complained impatiently, "The trouble with you, Sargent, is that you don't know what you want." "No," the painter answered. "The trouble, Mr. President, is that you don't know what a pose means." T. R., who was going up the stairs, turned, grasped a newel post, and roared, "Don't I!" And that is how he still stands in the Sargent portrait, now in the Red Room. When the painting was finished, the irrepressible Roosevelt declared, "I like his picture enormously," but Sargent complained to the press about T. R., and said that he had "felt like a rabbit in the presence of a boa constrictor." The painter swore that he would never do another presidential portrait. Fate was against him. In 1915, with the First World War raging, the British Red Cross held an auction in London at which the highest bidders received the right to have their portraits done by some of the world's greatest painters. The right to a portrait by Sargent was won for £10,000 by Sir Hugh Lane, the director of the Irish National Gallery. That was in April, and in May, Sir Hugh was one of those lost when the *Lusitania* was sunk by a German submarine. When his estate was finally settled, the United States had just entered the war; the Irish National Gallery, given the right to decide on the sitter for the Sargent portrait, chose President Woodrow Wilson.

Sargent could not very well refuse the request, and in October, 1917, he began the painting. He found Wilson stiff, dull, and boring. The portrait—it hangs in the Irish National Gallery—was acclaimed, but Sargent had wryly written to his old Boston friend, Isabella Stewart Gardner, "It takes a man a long time to look like his portrait . . . but Wilson is doing his best." Again he swore never to paint another President. This time he made it stick. In 1924, Calvin Coolidge, wishing to have his portrait done by Sargent, approached the painter through Sargent's close friend and cousin, Mary Potter. One night after dinner when Sargent was in a particularly good mood, she casually mentioned the President's request. Sargent fell back as though struck by a bullet, and cried, "You've ruined my whole dinner!" President Coolidge was never painted by John Singer Sargent.

—D. G. L.

BROTHERLY LOVE
among the
Founding Fathers

DRAWN FOR AMERICAN HERITAGE BY MICHAEL RAMUS

John Adams on Thomas Jefferson:	*"[He has] a mind, soured, yet seeking for popularity, and eaten to a honeycomb with ambition, yet weak, confused, uninformed, and ignorant."*
—on Alexander Hamilton:	*"This man is stark mad, or I am." "[Consider] the profligacy of his life; his fornications, adulteries and his incests."*
—on Benjamin Franklin:	*"His whole life has been one continued insult to good manners and to decency. . . . From five complete years of experience of Dr. Franklin . . . I can have no dependence on his word. . . . I wish with all my soul he was out of public service."*
Thomas Jefferson on Adams:	*"[He is] distrustful, obstinate, excessively vain, and takes no counsel from anyone."*
—on Hamilton:	*"I will not suffer my retirement to be clouded by the slanders of a man whose history, from the moment at which history can stoop to notice him, is a tissue of machinations against the liberty of the country which not only has received and given him bread, but heaped its honors on his head."*
Alexander Hamilton on Jefferson:	*"A man of profound ambition and violent passions . . . the most intriguing man in the United States . . . the intriguing incendiary, the aspiring turbulent competitor . . . prone to projects which are incompatible with the principles of stable and systematic government."*
—on Adams:	*". . . disgusting egotism . . . distempered jealousy . . . ungovernable indiscretion." ". . . vanity without bounds."*
Benjamin Franklin on vituperation:	*"Love your Enemies, for they tell you your Faults."*

Compiled by Robert C. Alberts